香港歷史考察之旅
Hong Kong History Excursion

港島區
Hong Kong Island

鄭寶鴻 著
Cheng Po Hung

商務印書館

香港歷史考察之旅：港島區

作　　者：鄭寶鴻
前言翻譯：Richard J. Smith
責任編輯：張宇程
美術設計：趙穎珊
出　　版：商務印書館 (香港) 有限公司
　　　　　香港筲箕灣耀興道 3 號東滙廣場 8 樓
　　　　　http://www.commercialpress.com.hk
發　　行：香港聯合書刊物流有限公司
　　　　　香港新界荃灣德士古道 220-248 號荃灣工業中心 16 樓
印　　刷：中華商務彩色印刷有限公司
　　　　　香港新界大埔汀麗路 36 號中華商務印刷大廈 14 字樓
版　　次：2023 年 2 月第 1 版第 2 次印刷
　　　　　©2019 商務印書館 (香港) 有限公司
　　　　　ISBN 978 962 07 5822 5
　　　　　Printed in Hong Kong
　　　　　版權所有　不得翻印

Hong Kong History Excursion: Hong Kong Island

Author:　　　　　Cheng Po Hung
Translator to
introduction:　　 Richard J. Smith
Executive editor:　Chris Cheung
Art design:　　　 Cathy Chiu
Publisher:　　　　The Commercial Press (H.K.) Ltd.,
　　　　　　　　8/F, Eastern Central Plaza, 3 Yiu Hing Road, Shau Kei Wan, Hong Kong
　　　　　　　　http://www.commercialpress.com.hk
Distributor:　　　The SUP Publishing Logistics (H.K.) Ltd.,
　　　　　　　　16/F, Tsuen Wan Industrial Centre, NT, Hong Kong
Printer:　　　　　C & C Offset Printing Co. Ltd.,
　　　　　　　　14/F, C & C Building, 36 Ting Lai Road, Tai Po, New Territories, Hong Kong

©2019 The Commercial Press (H.K.) Ltd.
First Edition, Second printing, February 2023
ISBN: 978 962 07 5822 5
Printed in Hong Kong

目錄

Contents

序

　　2000 年，香港大學通識教育部主管陳載澧教授賜電約見在下，討論由我來講述有關「昔日香港」之講座的可行性，並輔以三次包括港島中西區、東區以及九龍區街道和名所舊蹟的考察之旅，並着我設計步行路線。

　　當時，我正在編寫由三聯書店出版的有關港島、九龍及新界街道系列拙著，故有不少可供參考的現成材料。

　　就在與陳教授會面的數天後，我將構思好的步行路線大綱，連同「昔日香港」之講座內容，以及大量可用作今昔對照的早期照片呈交陳教授省覽，幸運地旋即獲知照准實行。

　　在講座開展同時，亦蒙香港大學美術博物館邀約，舉行多個不同主題的演講，介紹早期香港社會面貌。因此，大學通識教育部的考察之旅中除學生外，亦有部分博物館人員及聽眾出席。

　　這次考察之旅所涉及的範疇，包括香港、九龍歷次填海、海岸線遷移、銀行、金融、娛樂、宗教、醫療、教育、新聞、軍事地帶、警政、天氣、飲食、工商業以至建築物等項目，題材亦算廣泛，因而有戰戰兢兢的感覺。

　　及至 2003 年至 2004 年，香港大學美術博物館將我於該館演講之部分內容，輯錄出版了《香江知味》、《香江風月》及《香江道貌》一共三本書，內容分別是有關香港早期飲食、娼妓和電車路風光，每次出版皆會舉辦展覽。同時，該館的博物館學會，亦要求我舉辦一次從石塘咀至筲箕灣的電車遊，逐一介紹拙著述及之景點及其他名所舊蹟。

　　兩年後，北京中央電視台來港拍攝《香港名街》特輯，亦邀請我作了一次電車遊，以及一次以中西區大小街道為主題的步行考察。2015 年，中央電視台又邀請我拍攝有關 1941 年至 1945 年香港淪陷期間的特輯，當中談及被改作日化名稱之街道，以及曾更改用途的建築物，包括被改作「香港佔領地總督部」的滙豐銀行大廈，被改作「憲兵隊本部」的現終審法院，及依次被改作「日軍指揮部」及「東亞酒店」的半島酒店等。他們亦專程前往拍攝被改作「豐國印刷工場」之北角商務印書館及其龐大廠房之北角原址。

較具特色的一次，是陳載灃教授着我陪同他以及由台灣來港的著名作家陳映真先生，進行一次中上環區考察，講述百多年來香港的華洋金融業，以及銀行業發展。

由 2001 年開始，賞面邀約在下舉辦步行考察以及電車遊和巴士遊的單位，包括公營部門、博物館和學術機構；有一次香港電台電視部亦隨團拍攝。

另一次具特色之懷舊遊，是步行中上環多條街道，懷緬百多年來的報館和印務館，還有皇后大道中及利源東街等早期報紙集散中心。出席者為籌辦中之香港新聞博覽館的多位骨幹成員，包括慕名已久的陳淑薇女士、陳早標先生等。

我亦十分高興目睹該博覽館於 2018 年 12 月 5 日，在原必列啫士街街市落成開幕，開始為市民服務。

過去十多年，考察之旅曾步行經過具特別主題和風格的街道里巷，包括銀行區的皇后大道中和德輔道中；華人金融和貿易區的文咸東、西街；刻製圖章的文華里；別名「花布街」的永安街；娼院區的水坑口街；塘西風月區的皇后大道西及山道；西洋紅燈區的春園街和駱克道等。

在九龍半島則包括尖沙咀九龍倉（海港城）；水警總部所在的麥當奴道（後易名廣東道）；兩旁榕樹密佈、早期被形容為「恍如鬼域」的羅便臣道（後易名彌敦道）；「蔴埭（油麻地）花國（娼院區）」的吳松街和廟街；還有早期為海旁馬路主要街道之差館街（即上海街）等多條街道。此外，亦包括九龍城及寨城區的大小街道。

至於途經的港九早期名所舊蹟，則有銀行金融機構、百貨店舖、工展場地、馬場、遊樂場、戲院、茶樓酒家、西餐食肆及茶餐廳、酒店、纜車、電車、火車和巴士總站、碼頭、船塢、貨倉、公用事業機構、工廠、街市、辦館、廟宇、教堂、學校，還有填海區和機場。

多年來，在下亦經常乘搭火車或巴士前往新界旅行、郊遊、野餐、探親，以及新春「行大運」。火車沿途所經的地區有大圍、沙田、馬料水（現大學站）、大埔、粉嶺、上水及羅湖等。

　　而巴士途經的主要路線青山公路，所經的地區則有葵涌、荃灣、深井、青山酒店、容龍別墅、青山寺、青山灣、元朗、新田及錦田等。

　　對於上述新界區的街道及名勝，在下仍有深刻印象及美好回憶。

　　現將往昔在港九市區之考察遊覽路線，以及所經歷之旅行、郊遊經驗，作一綜合性之分區分段逐一介紹，並配以歷史圖片及相關說明，冀能從另一角度呈現香港早期面貌，期望與有心人士一同走入時光隧道，進一步探索香港早期歷史。

路線一

中上環發展之旅

Route 1

Tour on the Development of Central and Sheung Wan District

前言

中上環遊蹤的起步點為銀行區的皇后大道中，該區是政治、金融和商業中心。

1841年1月26日，英國人佔領香港島後，決定以中環為市中心，旋即移山填海，闢建道路，在花園道以西名為「政府山」的山段，興建了包括輔政司署、郵局等政府部門及宗教場所。

同年6月14日，政府進行第一次土地拍賣，出售若干幅由皇后大道至德輔道中新填出的土地，當中包括現時滙豐銀行等建築物的所在。時至今日，這一帶仍為主要的銀行區和商業區。在這地段上的橫街，主要為畢打街及砵典乍街，還有十多條早期為「私家街」的窄巷式街道，包括戲院里、利源東街、利源西街、興隆街，以至名為「鴨蛋街」的永勝街等。

當局亦在此開闢包括雲咸街、閣麟街、卑利街及鴨巴甸街等多條登山道路。

該區為人所熟知的建築，為落成於1842年的中環街市，其以西的地段為華人商業和居住區，大量茶樓、酒家、食品及百貨商店在此創設。中環街市對面的山段，當年為華人聚居的「上市場」。稍後，上市場的華人被遷徙往太平山區。

建議可在新紀元廣場外稍作歇息，在附近著名小食店購買乾果、燕窩糕及蝦子扎蹄等傳統風味食品，大快朵頤。在此中上環交界點，可了解這一帶的趣事，包括得雲茶樓和附近大牌檔美食，以及碩果僅存的地下公廁等。

及至1851年底，一場大火迫使當局在威靈頓街以西仍為海邊馬路的皇后大道，進行第二次填海，並在永勝街和旁邊的廣源市集接壤處，闢建包括文咸東街、文咸西街、蘇杭街、永樂街、禧利街及摩利臣街等多條街道，造就包括南北行所在的華人商貿和金融區，不少知名銀行和大商行也是在此發迹。文咸西街一帶的南北行商氣勢顯赫，一直持續至和平後的1950年代。

接近南北行的「水坑口娼院區」酒樓妓館雲集，二十世紀初才被「塘西」的石塘咀取代。水坑口街西端為英軍升起第一面英國旗的「佔領角」（現荷李活道公園所在），其周遭為以太平山街為中心的太平山區，該區著名建築物為創立於1870年的東華醫院。

1894年，太平山區受到致命疫症侵襲，經歷一場徹底的重整，大部分不合衛生的樓房被清拆，多條街道因重整而消失。

Introduction

The starting point of the tour begins at the initial portion of Queen's Road Central which runs through the banking, political, financial and commerical centre of Hong Kong.

After the British authorities took possession of Hong Kong on January 26, 1841, they decided that the heart of the present-day Central District to be the hub of the City and went about with initial reclamation, road building and established the core of their administration at a hilly area somewhat west of the present-day Garden Road, known as "Government Hill". Various buildings were erected including the early Colonial Secretariat and other government and religious establishments.

On June 14 of the same year, the Government carried out the very first land auction by putting on the market several plots of land along the north side of Queen's Road, including the newly created (present-day) Des Voeux Road Central, from east to west and from the HSBC plot to the Central Market area. This initial auctioned area remains to this day the premier banking and commercial hub. Several side streets existed in the same area, namely Pedder Street, Pottinger Street and about more than ten narrow lanes which were labelled as

"private streets". These include Theatre Lane, Li Yuen Street East, Li Yuen Street West, Hing Lung Street and Wing Sing Street, nick-named and commonly known as "Egg Street".

In due course, the Government constructed or opened up several streets, including Wyndham Street, Cochrane Street, Peel Street, Aberdeen Street and various routes of access to the Mid and Upper Levels. Well known buildings include the first generation of Central Market (completed in 1842). The area west of the market became the commercial and residential areas for the local Chinese population and teemed with numerous teahouses, restaurants, small eateries and general goods shops. The hilly area opposite the Central Market also became a residential area for the Chinese inhabitants and was known as "Upper Market" or "Upper Bazaar". The Chinese population was later forced to relocate from Central to the Tai Ping Shan area.

At the end of 1851, as a result of a huge fire, the authorities went about the second phase of reclamation starting at an area west of Wellington Street and bordering coastline along Queen's Road Central, Wing Shing Street, the Kwong Yuen

Bazaar and the adjoining areas. Newly created or established streets include Bonham Strand, Bonham Strand West, Jervois Street, Wing Lok Street, Hillier Street, Morrison Street and various other streets giving rise to the prosperous "Nam Pak Hong" (Bonham Strand) cluster of well-known financial and trading establishments which prospered till the early 1950's.

Many restaurants and brothels flourished in the so-called "Possession Street Brothel area" which was near to the commercial centre of Nam Pak Hong. However, the red light district was superceded in the early 20th century by the up-and-ruining Shek Tong Tsui red light district. The Possession Point area (present-day Hollywood Road Park) became known as the Tai Ping Shan area centred around Tai Ping Shan Street. The famous Tung Wah Hospital was established in 1870. In May 1894, the area was devastated by the outbreak of a vicious bubonic plague which resulted in the demolition of most of the tenements and streets were reconstructed and some were obliterated.

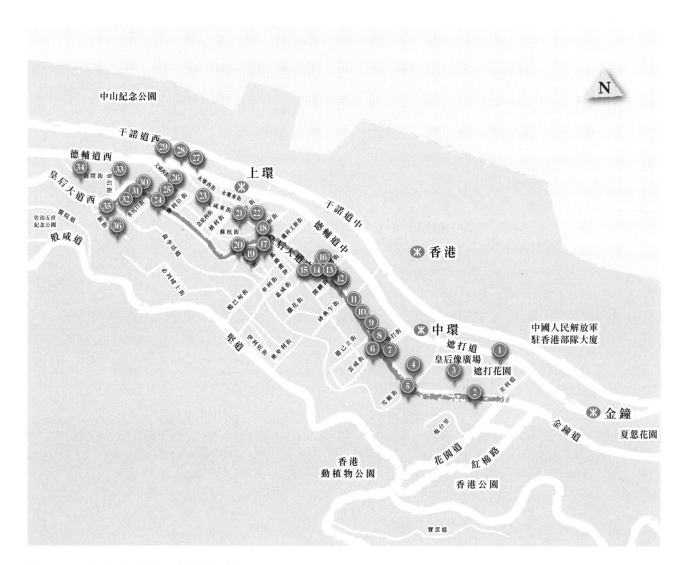

中山紀念公園

干諾道西

德輔道西

皇后大道西

佐治五世
紀念公園

殷咸道

堅道

⑳㉑㉗㉘㉙

㉞ ㉝

萬陸街 皇后街

③④ ㉚㉛㉜

醫院道

③⑥

永樂西街 永樂東街

文咸西街
文咸東街
乍畏街

蘇杭街

上 環 ⊛

干諾道中

德輔道中

干諾道中

德輔道中

香 港 ⊛

中 環 ⊛

遮打道

皇后像廣場

遮打花園

①

中國人民解放軍
駐香港部隊大廈

③

②

④

⑤

⑥⑦

⑧

⑨

⑩

⑪

⑫

⑬⑭⑮⑯

⑰⑱⑲⑳

㉑㉒

㉓

㉔㉕㉖

金 鐘 ⊛

金鐘道

夏愨花園

花園道

紅棉路

香港公園

香港
動植物公園

寶雲道

Please scan the below QR code for English map.

Palace of Government – Hongkong, China
Palais du Gouvernement

 由木球會（現遮打花園）西望第一代大會堂，約 1880 年。

其左方可見政府山及中上方的港督府（禮賓府）。大會堂的右鄰是原名「域厘行」的第一代滙豐銀行大樓。1841 年香港第一次填海，便是由大會堂左端，原為沿海小徑的皇后大道中，填至右端的海旁中（又名寶靈海旁中及海旁中道，1890 年代改名為德輔道中）。到了 1889 年展開的中西區大規模填海完成後，新海旁馬路則為干諾道中。該次由英王子干諾公爵（Prince Arthur, Duke of Connaught and Strathearn）奠基的填海基石，現時置於遮打花園（即圖中右下方）。

The City Hall and the HSBC building (first generation) of Praya Central (Des Voeux Road Central), looking from the Cricket Ground (now Chater Garden), c. 1880.

 由木球會望皇后大道中起點處，約 1926 年。

　　正中為早期名為「大草埔」及「操兵地」的美利操場，其左端的登山道路亦名為「大草埔馬路」。1860 年代，香港植物公園落成，該路段即改名花園道。操場的右鄰為政府山上的法國外方傳道會及於 1849 年落成的聖約翰座堂。右下方的部分大會堂於 1951 年建成中國銀行大廈，操場則於 1962 年建成希爾頓酒店，再於 1990 年代中拆卸，改建為長江集團中心。

Parade Ground and the Government Hill, c. 1926. The City Hall is on the bottom right.

1960 年的銀行區。

　　右中部可見正在興建的新大會堂，左下方為 1950 年代中落成的政府合署東座及中座。渣打銀行的背後是剛落成的於仁大廈（後來易名為太古大廈）的東翼。

The bank area of the Central District, c. 1960.

由皇后大道中 9 號望向正中的雪廠里（又名雪廠路，二十世紀初改名為雪廠街），1870 年代。

左方為炮台里口於 1845 年落成的雪廠（冰廠），曾被用作商場，後於 1958 年被改建成政府合署西座。右方於早期被編為皇后大道中 2 號、現時為成報中心的樓宇，曾依次為 1881 年開始服務的德律風（電話）公司、香港首間東藩匯理銀行之第二代行址，以及成立於 1918 年之東亞銀行第一代行址，亦曾被改建為萬國寶通（花旗）銀行大廈。

Ice House Street, looking from Queen's Road Central, c. 1870. The Ice House on the left is the Central Government Offices (West wing) nowadays.

 由雪廠街東望炮台里（右）及皇后大道中（左），約 1930 年。

炮台里是登上政府山及通往纜車站的主要道路。正中的大樹於數年前才倒下，大樹後是於 1870 年代落成的第一代柏拱行。帶有騎樓的建築是渣打銀行，其西鄰位於 5 號的建築是成立於 1891 年的發鈔銀行中華匯理銀行，稍後改建為法國東方匯理銀行。最左面的是位於 7 號的香港第二間發鈔銀行有利銀行。

Queen's Road Central and Battery Path (right), c. 1930. The Mercantile Bank is on the left.

 從皇后大道中上望雲咸街（「賣花街」），約 1925 年。

左方為於 1924 年前落成的亞細亞行，其前身於 1860 年代曾為第四間發鈔銀行「呵加剌」銀行（Agra Bank）。背後的山段上，約現藝穗會所在，早期為船政官畢打上尉（Lieutenant William Pedder）的官邸。右方的樓宇曾為第一代香港會，背後金字塔屋頂者是「比照」戲院（Bijou Cinema）。兩者於 1931 年改建為冷氣開放的娛樂戲院。背後位於 3 號的南華早報社現時為南華大廈。

Wyndham Street, looking from Queen's Road Central, c. 1925. The buildings on the right are the old Hong Kong Club and the Bijou Cinema, where the today's Entertainment Building situated.

Queen's Road.

 由雲咸街東望皇后大道中，約 1930 年。

右方為亞細亞行，現時為中滙大廈。左方為畢打街口，位於皇后大道中部分之香港大酒店，於
1909 年重建，其樓下為連卡佛公司。該酒店後於 1950 年代後期改建為中建大廈。正中有三角簷篷者
是面向都爹利街的丫士打酒店（Astor Hotel），所在現為公爵大廈。中部為政府山。

Queen's Road Central, looking east from Wyndham Street. The Government Hill is in the middle.

從畢打街口西望皇后大道中，約 1935 年。

煤氣燈的左邊是亞細亞行，背後是氣派一流的娛樂戲院；過了德忌笠街（德己立街）是安樂園飲冰室。右方是由第二代郵政總局及高等法院改建，於 1924 年落成的華人行，樓下面向交通指揮亭者是美利權餐室。

Queen's Road Central, looking west from Pedder Street, c. 1935. The China Building is on the right.

255   Queen's Road, Hongkong,

 約 1915 年的皇后大道中。

　　右方是 1909 年由中環街市前端 (現為恒生銀行) 遷至的香港影畫戲院,旁邊的橫街亦因而定名為
戲院里。右方的第二代高等法院舊址亦被用作影畫戲院。兩者於 1924 年分別改建為皇后戲院及華人
行。大樹後的洛興行 (現為萬邦行) 內有生產汽水的威建藥房。左邊德忌笠街口的樓宇,亦曾為香港大
藥房以及生產汽水的屈臣氏藥房所在,稍後改為安樂園飲冰室。圖中右方於 1841 年填海獲致的地段
上,有 13 條由戲院里開始,包括昭隆街、利源東街、利源西街、永安街、永吉街迄至鴨蛋街 (永勝街)
的橫街,早期為「私家街」,二十世紀初起由政府管理。

Queen's Road Central, c. 1915. The Hong Kong Theatre and Theatre Lane are on the right.

10　重建落成於 1961 年的皇后戲院及所在的陸海通大廈，2003 年。

皇后戲院於 2007 年被拆卸，後改建為商業大廈。

Queen's Theatre on no. 31, Queen's Road Central and Theatre Lane (right), 2003.

由昭隆街西望皇后大道中，約 1950 年。

右方為位於 37 號的著名百貨公司龍子行及龍光行，左方為中華百貨公司，其西鄰為永生、任玲記及大信珠寶金行。大信的樓上曾為中國日報社。

Queen's Road Central, looking west from Chiu Lung Street, c. 1950. The tallest building on the left is the Chinese Emporium Company.

開闢於 1845 年，以首任港督砵甸乍 (Henry Pottinger) 命名的砵典乍街，約 1949 年。

街上鋪上大量石板以便馬匹行走，因而又名為「石板街」，前面為皇后大道中。正中為於 1945 年和平後，由鵝頸橋遷至的鏞記酒家。石級底下有一所闢建於 1914 年的地下公廁（現已封閉），圖中可見現仍存在的公廁煙囪狀透氣管。

Pottinger Street, looking from Queen's Road Central, c. 1949. The Yung Kee Restaurant (fourth generation) is in the middle.

11 | 12

 由閣麟街西望皇后大道中，約 1905 年農曆新年期間。

　　左方有多間洋貨、鐘錶店及茶樓茶居，其中位於 112 號的均泰洋貨店，於 1930 年代後期改為永隆銀號。右下方為中環街市的入口梯道，西鄰租庇利街口是著名的南興隆辦館。前中部可見一輛行駛中之馬車，後方為一座新年慶典牌樓。

　　Queen's Road Central during the Lunar New Year, c. 1905. The Central Market and Jubilee Street are on the right.

(14) 由中環街市上望閣麟街，約 1930 年。

閣麟街以 1840 年代海軍中將閣麟 (Thomas Cochrane) 命名，其官邸位於此街與威靈頓街交界的上端。因有多間出售雀鳥的店舖，所以又別名「雀仔街」。正中煤氣燈的右邊，為被稱作「為食街」的一段士丹利街，這一帶開埠初期為華人聚居的「上市場」。大部分位於此街右邊的樓宇於 1992 年被拆卸，以興建登山扶手電梯。

Cochrane Street, also known as "Bird Shop Street", looking from Queen's Road Central, c.1930.

15 正在興建登山扶梯的閣麟街，
1992 年。

左方華潤百貨所在的僑商大廈正在
拆卸改建，以配合 1993 年落成的半山扶
手電梯。

Cochrane Street, on where
the pedestrian escalator was being
constructed, 1992.

16 由中環街市旁的租庇利街西望皇后
大道中，約 1935 年。

左方嘉咸街口的第一代高陞茶樓
外，有同一集團之東方戲院的廣告。正
中「利安鐘表行」的招牌後為第一代蓮香
茶樓。右方之梁新記百貨及慶雲茶樓兩
旁，為「工業原料街」之稱的同文街，以
及被稱為「花布街」的永安街。

Queen's Road Central, looking west
from Jubilee Street, c. 1935. Graham Street
is on the left.

路線一 中上環發展之旅　Route 1 Tour on the Development of Central and Sheung Wan District　**21**

6 Street Scene H. K.

17 闢建於 1840 年代初，以英國外交大臣鴨巴甸勳爵（George Hamilton-Gordon, 4th Earl of Aberdeen）命名的鴨巴甸街，約攝於 1930 年。

鴨巴甸街曾為「華洋居民分隔線」。當時這一帶已為華人商住區，有包括和昌及左方之杭州兩間影樓。和昌布招的右端為太昌茶樓，稍後改為襟江酒家，再約於 1980 年改為第二代蓮香茶樓。左中部有位於威靈頓街的冠南酒樓，其對面為一品陞酒家，該地段於 1996 年起為第三代蓮香茶樓。

Aberdeen Street, looking from Queen's Road Central. The place in the middle left is where the nowadays Lin Heung Teahouse situated.

 約 1915 年，由鴨巴甸街東望皇后大道中。

　　左中部可見於 1900 年開業，位於 172 號的先施洋貨疋頭的招牌。其西鄰位於 176 號、門前有救火水車的一列樓宇，為五號差館（警署）及「水車館」（消防局）。右方涉趣園茶煙室（鴉片煙館）招牌旁的舖位，曾為 1907 年在此開業的永安公司。位於圖正中為約於 1880 年開業的得雲茶樓，茶樓的一部分橫跨了永勝街的入口。1841 年的填海工程的西端便是填至被稱為「鴨蛋街」的永勝街。現先施公司所在伸延至威靈頓街的舊樓仍保留著，而永安公司的所在現時為華僑永亨銀行。在永勝街口的得雲茶樓原址，於 1992 年闢建成新紀元廣場的噴水池。

Queen's Road Central, looking west from Aberdeen Street, c. 1915. The no. 5 Police Station and the Fire Station were situated in the middle left.

⑲ 由位處中、上環的得雲茶樓西望上環皇后大道中，約 1925 年。

左方為現已遷入香港歷史博物館內、位於 180 號的老牌藥店誠濟堂，其東鄰為威靈頓街。其西鄰位於 182 號的美利權餐室分店於 1930 年改作二天堂藥行。

1851 年 12 月 28 日發生的一場大火，便是由這段尚為沿海的皇后大道，一直焚燒至國家醫院和修打蘭街一帶。當局事後在右邊的斜坡及海面填海，在新填地上建成右面的樓宇，以及開闢包括蘇杭街、文咸街、孖沙街及永樂坊（街）等多條街道。

Queen's Road Central, looking west from Wellington Street. On 28 December 1851, a huge fire broke out from here to the area near today's Sutherland Street in Sai Ying Pun. The district was quickly rebuilt after a reclamation.

從威靈頓街西望皇后大道中（左）、蘇杭街（中）及文咸東街（右），約1925年。

直至約1980年，蘇杭街的中文名稱仍為「乍畏街」。長期以來，這一帶被名為「十字路口」（Cross Roads）及「狗孖唪」，中心點為正中的交通指揮亭。蘇杭街為著名的綾羅綢緞街，文咸東街及孖沙街則為華人金融及商貿街。左方的百年大樓於1960年代中拆卸，年多後改建為啟豐大廈。

Traffic pavilion on the centre of the "cross roads" area, among Queen's Road Central (left), Jervois Street (middle) and Bonham Strand (right), c. 1925.

由文咸東街西望乍畏街（蘇杭街），約1935年。

可見多間綾羅綢緞、蘇杭布疋以及西裝女服店舖，亦有出售雜貨器皿以至燕窩者。正中有危樓支撐竹棚處是孖沙街。

Cotton, wool, silk and piece goods shops on both sides of Jervois Street, c. 1935.

從中上環交界「十字路口」望文咸東街華人金融區，約1930年。

右方的斜坡段於開埠初期為華人區的「廣源市集」，圖右方的祐記銀號，以及左方的振威鐘錶兩旁，曾有廣源東街及廣源西街。知名食府鏞記酒家便是於1942年在廣源西街始創。貞昌銀號的右鄰是1920年代初開業、位於11號的道亨銀號。該銀號於2013年變為星展銀行。這一帶現時為新紀元廣場及中遠大廈。

Chinese banks and bullion companies on Bonham Strand East, looking from Queen's Road Central, c. 1930. Jervois Street is on the left.

㉓ **由急庇利街東望文咸東街華人金融區中心點，1935 年 5 月。**

　　正中為慶祝英皇喬治五世（George V）加冕的牌樓，右方為金銀業貿易場的臨時行址。這一帶有包括源通利、誠信、麗興、永盛隆等多家著名金號。牌樓左方的時來遮廠，其東主應雁庭先生於 1960 年代為金銀業貿易場理事長。

Commenoration archway on Bonham Strand East, a Chinese bullion company area, to celelrate the Silver Jubilee of King George V.

㉔ **從皇后大道中及摩利臣街上望上環東街，1958 年。**

　　這條闢建於開埠初期、直達太平山區中心點的橫街，一直以來都是華人的市集街，圖中可見不少酒莊、醬園、米舖等。左方的大押後端有一實用喇叭筒（擴音機）店。右方為戰前開業的日南茶樓，其入口大堂為一穗豐米店。圖正中有一成衣大樓店，於農曆盂蘭節循例會於舖前舉辦「木頭公仔（木偶）大戲」表演，以娛坊眾。這部分東街於 1980 年代初改築為石級路段。

The "Market Street", Tung Street, Sheung Wan, looking from Queen's Road Central, 1958.

23 | 24

 1989 年，由皇后大道中下望摩利臣街。

　　右邊的舊樓稍後被拆卸重建。左下方可見位於「十王殿廣場」的公廁，數年後被拆以闢建上環文化廣場。公廁右方為以凌晨四時開市馳名的老牌茶樓清華閣；其背後是銀龍酒家，稍後改名為至好酒家。1990 年代，兩者被改建為安泰金融中心。

Morrison Street, looking from Queen's Road Central, 1989. Two traditional Chinese restaurants were situated in the middle left.

(26) 上環「十王殿廣場」，約 1922 年。

　　右方文咸東街上的浩昌瓷器西鄰是南便上環街市。正中的棚篷果攤處稍後興建公廁。左方為永樂東街，人力車旁是平香茶樓。與摩利臣街交界的吉祥茶居，稍後遷往鴨巴甸街雅麗氏醫院的舊址，原址改建為如意茶樓，約於 1928 年易名為清華閣。

The Sheung Wan public square located in the area between Wing Lok Street East (left) and Bonham Strand East (right), c. 1922.

 由德輔道西東望「南北行街」(文咸西街),約 1925 年農曆新年期間。

　　所有行商的店舖皆懸掛書有東主姓氏及店號的紙燈籠 (潮籍人士) 或精巧宮燈 (廣府人士),一片昇平景象。此種興建於十九世紀中期之典型南北行樓宇,現時只餘下位於 12 號的百昌堂一座。

Chinese medicine and rice shops on Bonham Strand West, during Lunar New Year, c. 1925.

 由文咸街望向位於德輔道西 9 號的老牌天發酒家，1986 年。

這家以潮州魚翅馳名的食府，為南北行商及其高層的食堂及外賣供應者，久享盛譽。可惜於 1980 年代後期結業拆卸。右方為天佐堂藥行。

Tin Fat Chiu Chow Restaurant on no. 9 Des Voeux Road West, looking from Bonham Strand West, 1986.

 由德輔道西天發酒家望向「南北行街」（文咸西街），約 1955 年。

部分南北行名店已他遷，不過此街仍維持其「駕勢」氣派。圖左方為天佐堂，右方為以「脆皮燒鵝」馳譽的公團飯店，亦為南北行老闆的食堂。天佐堂及右邊百安堂的「南北行街」行人路上，分別各有一小販檔售賣鮮蛋豆漿、油條，以及白果清心丸鴨蛋糖水，全為令人難忘的美食。

Bonham Strand West, looking east from Tin Fat Chiu Chow Restaurant, c. 1955.

28 | 29

 由水坑口街及皇后大道中、皇后大道西交界北望文咸東街，約 1920 年。

　　1841 年 1 月 26 日，英軍就在此登陸佔領港島。1851 年發生大火之前，這一帶仍為海段。圖左的煤氣燈旁是文咸西街，燈後是成立於 1868 年的南北行公所。正中為永樂街的永利威酒莊及平香茶樓。

Bonham Strand East, looking north from Queen's Road West, c. 1920. Bonham Strand West is on the left.

(31) 位於皇后大道中、水坑口街與摩羅下街（右）交界，於1920年代開業的富隆大茶廳（茶樓），1977年。

該茶廳在戰前的顯赫時期，有稱為「歌姬」的女伶獻藝，以及提供名為「茶花」的女侍應款客。

Foo Lung Teahouse at the junction of Queen's Road Central (left), Possession Street (front) and Lower Lascar Row, (right), 1977.

32 由皇后大道中、皇后大道西交界上望水坑口街，1977 年。

此街原為一大水坑。1841 年，英軍沿此水坑旁登上右邊一座被稱為「佔領角」的小山崗，宣示佔領港島。此街早期名為「下荷李活道」，1890 年代改名為波些臣街 (Possession Street)，稍後中文名改為水坑口街。從左邊兩三間花店樓上的「走馬騎樓」，仍可感受到二十世紀初「水坑口風月區」的餘韻。右方月利蔴雀耍樂的店舖所在，早期為於 1880 年代開業的宴瓊林酒家，其對上可見現仍營業之朱榮記的招牌。

Possession Street, looking from Queen's Road West, 1977.

⑶3 **從皇后街（早期又名和興西街）東望皇后大道西，1994年。**

　　左方有騎樓柱的三層唐樓，是著名涼果店任合興。其右方為以魚麵馳名的潮州飯店斗記，以及興記。其樓上亦為名店尚興，旁邊是潮州食肆林立，有包括兩興及陳勤記的「潮州巷」（又名香馨里）。其以西一帶的樓宇稍後全被清拆，後建成住宅屋苑帝后華庭。

Queen's Road West, looking east from Queen's Street, 1994. The famous "Chiu Chow eating house street", Heung Hing Lane, is in the middle.

 由修打蘭街東望著名的西營盤皇后大道西「雀仔橋」，1989年。

　　1851年的一場大火，就是由威靈頓街焚燒至這一帶。被稱為「雀仔橋」的堤道，築於開埠初期，供市民前往國家醫院就診。堤道底下有一所築建於1911年的地下公廁，約於千禧年後才停用。圖左於1851年時仍為海段，新填地上曾依次築建貨倉、戲院及華人樓宇。迄至1970年代，這一帶為「故衣」中心，現時左方碩果僅存的合德故衣行仍在營業。

"Bird's Bridge" (a causeway to Civil Hospital) on the side of Queen's Road West, Sai Ying Pun, 1989.

由保良局新街（新街）望向上環區，1870 年代中期。

右中部的佔領角已改作休憩場所「大笪地」，其左鄰面向鋤斷山街（1890 年代被併入荷李活道）的樓宇，早期為法國酒店，1874 年颶風後曾被用作臨時國家醫院。其左方為皇后大道西。

Sheung Wan area, looking from New Street, mid 1870s. Queen's Road West is on the left. The Possession Point, the nowadays Hollywood Road Park, is in the middle right.

36 約 1890 年的上環太平山區。

　　左下方為東華醫院，左中部為大笪地。圖中前方為磅巷，其左中部則為太平山街的百姓廟，以及由普樂戲園改建的大樓。該大樓戰後曾用作東華醫院門診部。這區的大部分樓房於 1894 年疫症後被全部清拆。

Tai Ping Shan area, c. 1890. Tung Wah Hospital and Possession Point are on the lower left.

路線二

中上環海旁演變之旅

Route 2

Tour on the Costal Development of Central and Sheung Wan District

前言

香港第一次填海,是在港島一條海旁小徑對開,一大段海邊斜坡旁開展。該小徑於 1842 年闢成皇后大道,而中區的沿海新道路,則名為海旁中、海旁中街或寶靈海旁中。到了 1890 年代中易名德輔道中。

開埠初期,位於海旁中的著名建築有顛地洋行及域厘行,所在現為置地廣場及滙豐銀行,還有第一代大會堂、中環街市及其西鄰的鐵行輪船公司大樓。

當時,由皇后大道中通往海旁中的主要道路,為畢打街及砵典乍街。到了 1887 年再闢成位於中環街市兩旁的域多利皇后街和租庇利街。中環街市亦同時重建,第三代中環街市落成於 1895 年,為這一帶的新地標。

中環街市以西,有包括興隆街、同文街、永安街及機利文街等多條早期為「私家街」的橫街,內外有不少貨倉、機器工場、經營船具和雜貨等的店舖,到了二十世紀才逐漸轉營他業。

整條海旁中,除畢打和雪廠等碼頭外,亦有多座屬於各沿海商行私自興建的碼頭。

1889 年展開的中西區大規模填海完成後,新闢了一條以填海主催者遮打爵士 (Sir Catchick Paul Chater) 命名的遮打道。在道路正中興建一座寶亭,置放維多利亞女皇像,並在此闢築皇后像廣場,於 1896 年落成,慶祝女皇登位 60 週年鑽禧。遮打道兩旁及毗連干諾道中的新辦公大樓,幾全為置地公司擁有。

當時被稱為「海皮」新海旁馬路的干諾道中,自 1900 年起陸續有 30 多座碼頭落成,大部分為停泊內河輪船、港澳輪渡及渡海小輪,還有不少往來世界各地的大洋船。此外,亦有多座供「嘩啦嘩啦」(電船仔) 碇泊的小碼頭。

1951 年,開闢愛丁堡廣場的填海工程展開,再經歷往後的多次中上環填海後,干諾道中的沿海地位逐漸被其他新道路取代。

Introduction

The first reclamation project undertaken by the authorities began with a small path along the northern coastline of the present-day Central District.

In 1842, this path became known as Queen's Road which served as Central's (Victoria City) new main street. This stretch of road was also called Praya Central, Praya Central Street or Bowring Praya Central. In 1890, the road became known as Des Voeux Road Central.

In the early days of the territory, well-known buildings along the Praya Central were Dent & Co. and Wardley House near the present-day Hong Kong Landmark and the HSBC Building. There were also the first generation of "City Hall", the Central Market and the P&O Headquarters Building (Peninsula and Orient Steam Navigation Company). Pedder Street and Pottinger Street were the main links between Queen's Road Central and Praya Central. In 1887, newly constructed Queen Victoria Street and Jubilee Street bordered "Central Market" which saw its third-generation version completed in 1895 and soon became the area's new landmark. The rebuilt market was a three-storey Victorian-style structure with a tower in the middle.

Streets west of Central Market included Hing Lung Street, Tung Man Street, Wing On Street and Gilman Street, and various neighbouring lanes and side-streets were considered as private streets. These streets saw the rise and flourishing of machinery and mechanical workshops, shops dealing in shipping accessories and general goods stores, and these establishments carried out their businesses as such until the early 20th century when other trades and businesses took over.

Apart from the Pedder Pier and the Ice House Street Pier, there existed quite a number of privately-built piers serving mainly shipping establishments along Praya Central.

After the completion of the vast reclamation projects in Central and Western District in 1889, Chater Road was constructed in honour of Sir Paul Chater, the mastermind behind the major reclamations in Central and Victoria Harbour. At the centre of Chater Road, there stood a statue of Queen Victoria enthroned beneath a domed cupola. The statue was commissioned to commemorate her Diamond Jubilee in 1897 and was completed in 1896. The statue dominated the then called Statue Square. The heart and environs of Chater Road and Connaught Road Central soon became the property of Hong Kong Land.

In the early 1900's, the newly constructed Connaught Road Central saw the completion of 30 or more piers catering to the needs of inner harbour shipping, HK-Macao ferries, cross harbour ferries and ocean lines. There also existed smaller piers used by mini cross harbour ferries or motor boats known as "walla-walla".

The year 1951 saw the initiation of the reclamation of Edinburgh Place and with the subsequent reclamation schemes along the coastline of Central and Sheung Wan, the significance of Connaught Road Central for shipping was superceded by other road and pier constructions.

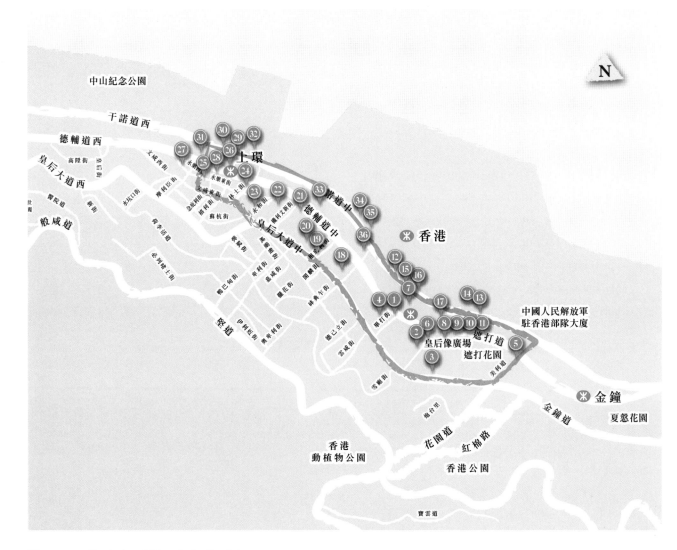

Please scan the below QR code for English map.

1926 年 1 月 1 日元旦，畢打街與正中德輔道中交界的香港大酒店發生大火。

灌救水喉噴射圖正中畢打街的地段，為 1841 年填海前的原有海旁。左方為由第二代郵政總局及由高等法院改建的華人行，頂樓懸掛五色國旗的南唐酒家，約於三年後易名為大華飯店。

The Hong Kong Hotel was on fire in 1926. The middle part of the hotel is the original waterfront in 1841 before Hong Kong's first reclamation.

Hongkong Hotel, Hongkong.

48

中環海岸線的海旁中,約 1882 年。

左方樓宇是原為域厘行 (Wardley House) 的第一代滙豐銀行大樓。正中是由顛地洋行改建,於 1867 年開業的香港大酒店,在畢打街隔鄰的是渣甸行。圖右的海段現為皇后像廣場及終審法院所在,可見數名乘坐轎子及人力車的「洋大人」或「大班」。

Praya Central (Des Voeux Road Central), c. 1882. The HSBC Building (first generation) is on the left. The Hong Kong Hotel and Jardine House are in the middle.

1874 年 9 月 22 日,海旁中經歷了一場被形容為「猛烈轟炸」的颶風。

海面滿佈翻沉的船艇,滿目瘡痍。右上方可見第一代滙豐銀行大樓(右)和大會堂(左)。

Praya Central, after a fatal typhoon on 22 September, 1874. The City Hall and HSBC building are on the right.

1891 年的中環寶靈海旁中(海旁中)。

正中六層高的建築是即將重建落成的香港大酒店(1926 年毀於大火)。過了畢打街是渣甸(怡和)洋行。最左面的建築是 1886 年落成的第二代滙豐銀行大廈,其前方正進行填海工程。位於大酒店前端的是歷史悠久的畢打碼頭。1890 年代中,寶靈海旁中易名為德輔道中。

Bowring Praya, c. 1891. The tallest building is the newly rebuilt Hong Kong Hotel. The Jardine House is on the right.

 由美利道望向德輔道中，約 1965 年。

正中的中國銀行大廈及落成於 1935 年的第三代滙豐大廈之部分地段，原屬第一代大會堂。左方為位於美利操場原址，落成於 1962 年的希爾頓酒店；右方為 1965 年改建的新太子大廈。

The Hilton Hotel and the bank area, Central District, c. 1965.

 約 1935 年的德輔道中。

雪廠街的左端為廣東銀行，右端為國民商業儲蓄銀行，其右鄰是 1935 年重建落成、位於 10 號的東亞銀行大廈。國民銀行背後位於雪廠街中部的樓宇，是香港股份總會（香港證券交易所前身）的股票交易場所。

The National Commercial and Savings Bank, and the Bank of East Asia on Des Voeux Road Central, c. 1935.

⑦ **1926年一場雨災後的德輔道中。**

　　右方為正在拆卸的香港大酒店，其左鄰依次為荷蘭安達銀行，即將落成的交易行（連卡佛大廈，電話公司所在）。正中三座三層高的樓宇，位於正中的一座是在 10 號的第二代東亞銀行行址。圓形屋頂的是 1924 年重建落成的廣東銀行。左方的亞力山打行樓下是屈臣氏大藥房。

Alexandra House (left), Bank of Canton (middle) and the demolishing Hong Kong Hotel (right) on Des Voeux Central, after a rainstorm, 1926.

 在新填地上開闢的皇后像廣場，約 1920 年。

可見遮打道正中花崗石寶亭內的維多利亞女皇像。其背後左方為第一代大會堂。三角屋簷內之皇室標誌的獨角馬，曾傳說「成精」到處奔跑而鬧得沸沸騰騰。右方為第二代滙豐銀行大樓，左邊的高等法院現時為終審法院大樓。

Statue Square, looking from the new waterfront, Connaught Road Central, c. 1920. The City Hall and HSBC building are at the back of the statue.

1954 年的皇后像廣場。

和平紀念碑旁是落成於 1897 年，由皇后大道中（現娛樂行所在）遷至的第二代香港會所。左方可見 1951 年開展之填海工程所獲得之愛丁堡廣場地段，其上正舉辦第十二屆工展會。其所在現為大會堂。

Hong Kong Club on Jackson Road, c. 1954. The Exhibition of Hong Kong Products is held on the Edinburgh Place just reclaimed.

 1962 年，由皇后像廣場（部分已被改作停車場）望向愛丁堡廣場。

可見同年落成的大會堂。1966 年，皇后像廣場重建為現時面貌。

Statue Square, temporarily used as a car park, and the newly opened City Hall, 1962.

由皇后像廣場西望遮打道，1960 年。

　　左方為第一代太子行，旗幟後方是德輔道中上的怡和大廈。右方為皇后行，於 1963 年改建成文華酒店。正中是聖佐治行，其背後是由沃行及皇帝行改建的於仁大廈。

Chater Road, looking west from Statue Square, 1960. The buildings from the right side are Queen's Building, St. George Building and the unfinished Union House respectively.

Hongkong Harbour.

 大致完成的中西區填海工程，約 1895 年。

左中部為德輔道中，其左旁兩層高建築的連卡佛公司，所在位置現時為創興銀行。右上方有塔樓者是落成於 1895 年的第三代中環街市。右前方的新海旁即將開闢成干諾道中。

The newly reclamation area of Central District, c. 1895. Des Voeux Road, Central (Bowring Praya) is on the left, and Connaught Road Central is being built on the right side.

Queen and Prince Buildings, Hongkong

13 1903 年的干諾道中。

　　左中部是落成於 1900 年、原名「雪廠街碼頭」的天星碼頭，其右方是 1899 年落成的皇后行（現為文華酒店），再隔鄰是 1903 年落成的太子行。右方正興建亞力山打行。圖中前方是 1901 年 5 月啟用的卜公碼頭，當時仍未有上蓋。

Star Ferry Pier and Blake Pier (right) on Connaught Road Central, 1903. Queen's Building and Prince's Building, which completed in 1899 and 1903 respectively, are at the back.

 位於干諾道,原為雪廠街碼頭的天星碼頭,約 1907 年。

碼頭頂部有油麻地蒸氣洗衣公司(位於窩打老道近廣華醫院)的廣告。右方可見早期的天星小輪。

Star Ferry Pier, c. 1907. The former name of the pier is "Ice House Street Pier".

約 1908 年的新海旁干諾道中。

　　當時已有若干座新建築物落成，包括左邊的皇帝行及萬順酒店。畢打街的另一端正興建郵政總局。再隔鄰是包括南清（華）早報所在之大樓、德忌利士船公司（現為中總大廈）。砵典乍街的右邊即將興建域多利戲院。中環街市前為簡陋的香港影畫戲院，一年後遷往皇后大道中與戲院里交界。

　　The new praya, Connaught Road Central, c. 1908. The King's Building and Mansion Hotel on Pedder Street are on the left. A simple structure cinema is on the right, in front of the Central Market.

Hongkong, Monument
of the Duke of Connaught.

約 1902 年至 1903 年間，豎立於干諾道中與畢打街交界的干諾公爵銅像，約 1915 年。

左方為萬順酒店，右方為第三代郵政總局（現為環球大廈），正中為香港大酒店（現為置地廣場）。

Statue of the Duke of Connaught, on Connaught Road Central and Pedder Street, c. 1915, surrounded by Mansion Hotel (left), Hong Kong Hotel and the General Post Office (right).

(17) 約 1926 年，由皇后像廣場西望干諾道中。

左邊的建築物依次為皇后行（現為文華酒店）、郵政總局、樓高七層的鐵行大廈等。正中為同年落成的滅火局（消防局）大廈。前方為一年前落成的皇后碼頭，後面為天星碼頭及卜公碼頭。泊有大洋船的是鐵行碼頭。

Connaught Road Central, c. 1926. The newly elected Queen's Pier is at the front. The Star Ferry Pier, the Blake Pier and the P&O Pier are next to it.

16 | 17

 即將拆卸重建的萬宜大廈，1995 年。

這座落成於 1957 年的大廈內，設有香港首批扶手電梯。大廈內有著名的紅寶石餐廳，以及早期位於右下端舖位的蘭香室茶餐廳，兩者皆為人所熟知。

The first generation Man Yee Building on Des Voeux Road Central, 1995.

 約 1947 年的德輔道中。

和平後第二年，市面正恢復興盛。右方為於日佔時代被改名為「中央市場」的中環街市，左方為消防局（現恒生銀行所在），其前面及電車的右面各有一輛載客三輪車。兩部電車之間的百年大樓於 1957 年改建為萬宜大廈。正中可見於 1931 年由香港大酒店改建之告羅士打行頂端之大鐘樓，其前方有尖塔建築者是第二代渣甸（怡和）洋行。

Des Voeux Road Central, looking east from Jubilee Street, c. 1947. The Fire Brigade Building is on the left, and the Central Market is on the right.

18｜19

HONG KONG,
STREET SCENE NEAR MARKET.

20 德輔道中望向租庇利街，約 1908 年。

　　這段由拆卸包括鐵行輪船公司大樓而開闢的租庇利街，連同左端的域多利皇后街，落成之時適值維多利亞女皇登位 50 週年金禧，故兩者分別以 Victoria 及 Jubliee 命名。人力貨車之後方為鐵行里。左前方紅磚大理石的第三代中環街市於 1895 年建成。

Jubilee Street, looking from Des Voeux Road Cental, c. 1908. The old Central Market is on the left.

21 出殯巡遊隊伍經過「電車路」（德輔道中），約 1930 年。

　　左方為昭平百貨公司，過了花布街（永安街）的天孫化妝品公司，所在現時為大生銀行大廈。介乎天孫公司與公昌押之間是機利文街。圖右方雲泉茶樓旁者則為機利文新街。

Funeral parade passing through Des Voeux Road Central, c. 1930. Gilman's Bazaars is on the right.

20 | 21

 約 1948 年的德輔道中。

　　左方的瑞興公司於 1958 年改建為第一代李寶椿大樓。過了永和街的先施公司現為南豐大廈。正中為消防局，右方的金龍酒家現時為金龍中心的一部分。右中部為位於永樂東街口兼售音響唱片的天壽堂藥行。

　　Intersection between Des Voeux Road Central and Wing Wo Street, c. 1948. Shui Hing Company and Sincere Company are on the left.

 由永和街西望德輔道中，1936 年。

左方有金龍酒家、翔鳳冰室及陶然飲冰室。右方為 1921 年在新填地上落成的新世界影戲院，正上映影片《荼薇香》及即將上映《午夜殭屍》。正中的永安公司大樓於 1972 年後才拆卸重建。

Des Voeux Road Central, looking west from Wing Wo Street, 1936. The World Theatre and Wing On Company are on the right.

24 **1929 年，由永安公司前東望德輔道中。**

右方為林士街，左方為位於 186 號的康年儲蓄銀行及人壽公司。其左鄰為怡園西菜館，約於 1933
年改建為金龍酒家。

Des Voeux Road Central and Rumsey Street (right), 1929. Hong Nin Savings Bank is on the left.

25 由北便上環街市（西港城）向東望上環電車總站，約 1935 年。

　　左方是摩利臣街及旁邊於 1927 年落成的皇后酒店。與干諾道中毗連的一長列樓宇，有多間「時租」旅館和客棧，使這一帶成了私娼麇集的「人肉市場」。中後方有塔型的建築的是大新百貨公司。右邊可見著名的雜貨店朱廣蘭，其西鄰為銀龍酒家。

The tramway terminal on Des Voeux Road Central, looking from Western Market, Sheung Wan, c. 1935. Some low-grade hotels and unlawful brothels were situated on the middle left.

26 由機利文街至摩利臣街之間的中上環海旁，1974 年。

干諾道中對開已有大片由 1955 年開始填築的新填地。在停車場背後的建築為重建中的永安公司。前方為港澳碼頭。右面一大部分土地於入夜後為販攤聚集之「平民夜總會」，較油麻地榕樹頭及廟街一帶更為熱鬧，所在現為信德中心及新港澳碼頭。永安大廈地盤左鄰的舊建築，是被稱為「船頭官」的海事處。上環街市（現為西港城）對開的海面正進行填海。

Seafront of Connaught Road Cental, between Gilman Street and Morrison Street, 1974.

27 約 1960 年的上環干諾道西，由東來里至皇后街的一段。

右方可見位於干諾道西與德輔道西「轉角位」的三角碼頭。中部最高者是位於 37 號的東山酒店。海邊泊有無數貨艇及躉船（我曾在多艘相連的貨艇上參加婚宴）。左面東來里口的一座唐樓現仍存在（我不時與考察團在其樓下於 1952 年開業的海安咖啡室「嘆西茶」，懷緬早期光景）。

由「船頭官」海事處至三角碼頭為止的一段干諾道中及干諾道西，加上其背後的德輔道中，迄至 1970 年代初為私娼活躍地帶。在干諾道「搵食」者被稱為「海皮貨」，在德輔道中者被稱為「企電車路」。到了 1970 年代中，兩街的旅館及客棧全被清拆，「交易陽台」消失殆盡，被稱為「人肉市場」的繁榮「娼盛」，亦告風流雲散；代之而起是炒賣往來港澳渡輪船票的「黃牛黨」。

Connaught Road West, from Tung Loi Lane to Des Voeux Road West, c. 1960. Wing Lok Street Wharf is on the extreme right.

 約 1928 年，由上環急庇利街東望干諾道中。

右面有多家便利華人客商的旅店和客棧。當時電車是經禧利街轉入德輔道中。左邊多座碼頭當中有禧利街對開的同安公司碼頭，供永安、東安及西安等多艘省港輪船停泊。

Chinese hotels and inns on Connaught Road Central, near Hillier Street and Cleverly Street (right), Sheung Wan, c. 1928.

㉙ 1927 年同安碼頭的景象。

碼頭左邊泊有東安渡輪。

Tung On Pier on Connaught Road Central near Hillier Street, 1927.

㉚ 1937 年 5 月，搭建於干諾道中與禧利街交界、慶祝英皇喬治六世（King George VI）加冕的牌樓。

右方的興發冰室於戰後改名為「虱二」（暗喻「風月無邊」）餐室，50 年代再改為中記中菜館。

An archway elected on Connaught Road Central to celebrate the coronation of the King George VI, May 1937.

(31) 約 1925 年，著名的「省港船」瑞泰號正停泊在位於干諾道西及永樂街對出，供「省港澳汽船公司」渡輪停泊的永樂街碼頭。

該碼頭稍後改名為永樂碼頭，因其位處馬路「轉角」點，所以又被稱為「三角碼頭」。附近地段亦被名為「三角碼頭」區，每年皆會舉行三角碼頭盂蘭勝會。

Ferry *Sui Tai*, services to Canton and Macao from Wing Lok Street Wharf, c. 1925.

(32) 約 1970 年的上環干諾道中。

港澳輪渡「澳門」號，正停泊於木結構的港澳碼頭。左方可見林士街停車場，其對面的多幢舊樓於三年後拆卸以興建新永安公司大廈。由禧利街至急庇利街之間仍可見多家旅館及客棧。

A Macao ferry besthed by the pier where the today's Macao Ferry Terminal located.

1937 年 9 月 2 日，一場造成超過一萬人死亡的風災後的干諾道中。

可見一艘船頭被吹上岸的大洋船。面向華商總會（中華總商會）的樓宇，現時為中華廠商會大廈。輪船的左方為消防局及統一碼頭。

A ship wrecked on Des Voeux Road Central near the United Pier, after a disastrous typhoon on 2 September, 1937.

 消防局（戰前名為滅火局）大廈對開之統一碼頭，約 1950 年。

該碼頭可供九條航線的渡輪停泊。正中為汽車渡輪，左方為往深水埗，右方為往旺角，以及包括荃灣、梅窩、坪洲、青山、東涌、沙螺灣及大澳等小輪航線。左中部可見一艘往深水埗的小輪及汽車渡輪。

United Pier on Connaught Road Central, c. 1950, where the today's International Finance Centre (phase one) situated.

 第二代卜公碼頭及海濱公園，約 1980 年。

1963 年，政府在愛丁堡廣場以西再進行填海，獲致現郵政總局及交易廣場的地段，又先後在最新的海旁興建曲尺型的第二代卜公碼頭及海濱公園。其所在現為中環機鐵站及國際金融中心。

Promenade of the Central District, and the second generation Blake Pier, c. 1980.

ONGKONG. (FROM THE SEA) 4:

36 約 1924 年的干諾道中。

正中為域多利皇后街口的油蔴地小輪碼頭,於 1933 年改建成統一碼頭。其背後是拆卸和平戲院後興建中的滅火局(消防局)大廈。其左鄰的樓宇於 1958 年及 1963 年拆卸,建成恒生銀行大廈(現為盈置大廈),以及聯邦大廈(現為永安集團大廈)。

Connaught Road Central, c. 1924. The Fire Brigade Building in the middle is in construction.

中西區半山懷舊遊

Route 3

Nostaglic Tour on Mid-levels of Central and Western District

前言

起步點為政府山一帶的花園道、炮台里，再沿雪廠街步上下亞厘畢道、堅道一帶的大街小巷，參觀這一帶的聖約翰座堂、輔政司署、港督府、會督府及天主教總堂等景點。亦會順道考察這一帶的報業發源地和當年報館的位置。

早期為西洋娼妓區的擺花街，於戰後為著名粵劇戲服街，連同聯接的荷李活道，於十九世紀後期起，有多間學塾和學校，當中包括早期為最高學府的皇仁書院。因此，有包括商務印書館等多間書坊舖（書店）在這一帶開設。

矚目的建築羣為中央警署的「大館」、裁判署和域多利監獄，其鄰近之士丹頓街，早期有多家被名為「菩薩舖」的尼庵及佛寺，因而又名為「師姑街」。六、七十年代起，漸被印務館取代。近年來，蛻變為一如蘭桂坊的「SOHO 區」。士丹頓街又被稱為「卅間」，此街的盛事為每年農曆七月由坊眾舉辦的「盂蘭勝會」超幽醮會。

「卅間」與必列啫士街地段上的樓宇，於淪陷時期曾被盜拆及戰火摧毀，和平後變成「卅間廢墟」。1950 年代初，多座唐樓、已婚警察宿舍及街市等，在廢墟上重建落成。該座街市於 2018 年底重新改建為香港新聞博覽館。

荷李活道早期亦有「文武廟直街」的別名。文武廟落成於 1847 年，其前端的廣場，以及開埠初期名為「佔領角」的「大笪地」，為最早的華人活動及休閒場所。

由文武廟迄至部分西營盤的地段，為華人聚居的太平山區，滿佈密集和衛生欠佳的樓房，中軸線為太平山街，附近有東華醫院及保良局，亦有兩間粵劇戲院。

1894 年，太平山區發生瘟疫，瞬即蔓延。當局後來將區內的樓宇全部拆卸，稍後在此開闢「市肺」卜公花園，興建現為香港醫學博物館的香港病理檢驗所，以及在 1918 年落成的第二代青年會大樓。

考察時可經過疫症前的街市街（普慶坊）尋找「太平山街市」及 1844 年第一間警署的遺址。還有位於上端般咸道遭受 1926 年雨災影響而遷至第四街（高街）的八號差館。行程也可經過又名「貓街」的摩羅上街，參觀文武廟及其公所，講述早期「斬雞頭、燒黃紙」的審案情況。期間可在對面的文武廟廣場稍事休息，然後往歌賦街、結志街及伊利近街的店舖或大牌檔，享受平民化美食。

Introduction

The starting point embraces the area around the Government House, the environs of Garden Road, treading down Battery Path, saunter up to Upper Albert Road, following which one explores the various lanes and side-streets along Caine Road. Then, swing down to admire the historical Saint John's Cathedral, the Central Government Offices, the Government House, the Bishop's House and the nearby Catholic Cathedral. At the same time, one may reminisce and check out Hong Kong's earliest flourishing newspaper trade and its various locations.

In the early years of the territory, brothels catering mostly to Westerners were located mainly around Lyndhurst Terrace. In the post-war period, there were numerous shops selling Cantonese opera paraphernalia. In the late 19th century, there existed in this area and along Hollywood Road numerous old Chinese-style learning centres and schools, including the renowned Queen's College (then known as The Government Central School) and thus giving rise to the establishment of various bookshops and printing companies.

Then we come to the most amazing complex of early Colonial-era buildings: the Central Police Station complex (revitalised as Tai Kwun), the Central Magistracy and the Victoria Prison. In nearby Staunton Street there used to exist a number of Buddhist/Taoist nunneries and other traditional places of worship. There were also several papier-mache or shops selling traditional Chinese paper offerings. Hence, the nickname of the street was "Nunnery Street". In the 1960's and 70's, several printing shops moved in. More recently, the area has transformed itself into SOHO (South of Hollywood Road), an offshoot of Lan Kwai Fong, Hong Kong's night-life hot spot. Staunton Street has also been known as "Sam Sap Kan" as there were thirty houses or tenements built on the street in the early days. An annual festival held in the Staunton Street area is the "Yu Lan Festival" (or Hungry Ghost Festival/ceremony) which takes place on the 14th (or later) day of the seventh month in the lunar calendar to appease the hungry wandering ghosts or spirits.

"Sam Sap Kan" and the neighboring Bridges Street suffered devastation during the Japanese occupation and remained a dilapidated area after the war.

The early 1950's saw the building of numerous Chinese-style Tong Lau, a police married quarters and the Bridges Street market (no. 2), a Bauhaus-style structure which opened in 1953. The market was transformed into Hong Kong's first news museum (News-Expo) in 2018.

Hollywood Road is also home to the famous Man Mo Temple completed in 1847. Prior to the building of the Temple, the site together with the neighboring Possession Point location came to be known as "Tai Tat Tei" (or "Dai Tat Tei"), literally meaning "large piece of land". The area served as the earliest venue for the purposes of a bazaar, recreational and entertainment hub for the local population.

West of the Man Mo Temple was the densely populated area known as "Tai Ping Shan" and was clustered around Tai Ping Shan Street. Nearby was the Tung Wah Hospital and Po Leung Kuk, plus two popular Cantonese opera theatres, Shing Ping and Tung Hong.

In May 1894, the Tai Ping Shan area was devastated by the outbreak of a vicious bubonic plaque which spread rapidly in the closely packed and unhygienic tenements. The authorities decided to demolish most of the tenements. In much of the area, the Blake Garden was set up (as a city lung), together with the Hong Kong Museum of Medical Sciences which is housed in the former old Pathological Institute. Finally, the second generation of the Chinese YMCA in Hong Kong was completed in 1918 (Bridges Street).

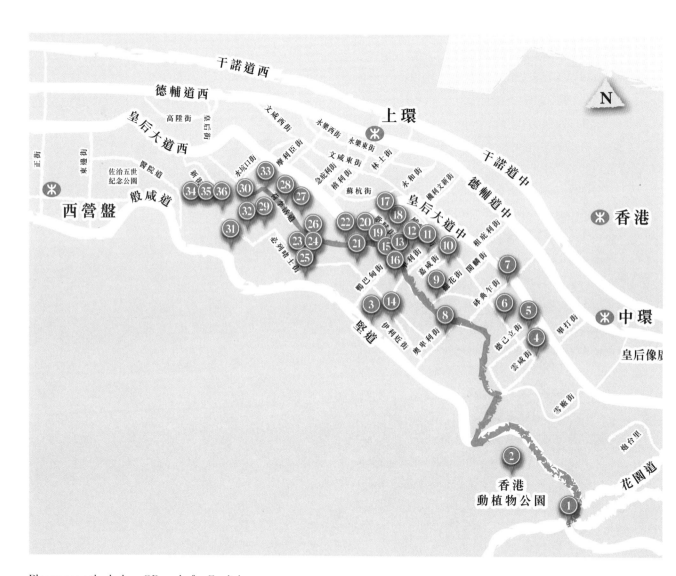

Please scan the below QR code for English map.

在當時，纜車不時因停止供電而停
駛。本明信片由日本書店發行，經過憲
兵隊檢閱。

A peak tram on Tramway Path near
Bowen Road, c. 1942, during the period of
Japanese occupation.

② 約 1960 年的香港植物公園（兵頭
花園）。

落成於 1930 年代的噴水池蓄養的
金魚十分吸引。背後為日據時期在港督
府（現為禮賓府）內加建的塔狀樓宇。

The fish pond in the Hong Kong
Botanical Garden, c. 1960.

 以 1844 年第一任警察裁判司威廉・堅（William Caine）命名而於同年闢成的堅道，約 1913 年。

左邊有石級的卑利街東鄰曾是九號警署所在，正中衞城道（早期名為炮台道）上的大樹左方的三角屋頂樓宇，於 1914 年改建為甘棠第（現中山紀念館所在）。右方的一列樓宇開有小祇園齋菜館，以及稍後以椰子糖及雪糕馳名的甄沾記。

Caine Road, c. 1913. The street on the left with stone steps is Peel Street.

④ 早期為報業街、又名「大鐘樓（位於畢打街）上街」的威靈頓街，約 1930 年。

左方為位於雲咸街 5 號，創辦於 1845 年的《德臣西報》《中國郵報》），其下鄰的雲咸街 1 至 3 號為《南華早報》。正中的騎樓下方，可見《華字日報》的招牌。左中部亦有一「電浪報局、代理廣東公評報」的招牌。

Wellington Street, looking from Wyndham Street, c. 1930.

3 | 4

（香港憲兵隊檢閱濟）　　　　　　　　　華人街風景

 約 1942 年日據時期，德忌笠街（德己立街）與士丹利街交界的服裝店與街頭小販攤檔。

在這張經檢閱發行的明信片中，可見部分顧客及市民仍為衣着光鮮者。這些販攤不少於 1941 年 12 月九龍淪陷初期開設。

Hawker stalls on D'Aguilar Street, c. 1942, during the Japanese occupation.

6 2002 年，位於中環威靈頓街 32 號
的鏞記酒家正慶祝成立六十週年。

可見當時酒家輝煌及耀目的裝飾。

Diamond jubilee decoration of Yung
Kee Restaurant on Wellington Street,
2002.

7 由皇后大道中上望砵典乍街（石板
街），約 1913 年。

轎子底下正興建一所地下公廁。這
一帶有若干間學塾和教館。正中「酒」字
招牌背後為杏讌樓西菜館，孫中山先生
曾在此會晤革命同志。再上方有三角屋
頂者是位於荷李活道 1 號，及宣惠里之
間的樓宇，於 1919 年改建為中央警署
「大館」新翼。

Pottinger Street, looking upward from
Queen's Road Central, c. 1913.

HONGKONG street life

 被稱為「長命斜」的奧卑利街，1981年。

左方為中央警署「大館」新舊翼，以及其上端的域多利監獄。戰後，「考車牌」（駕駛考試）的起點和終點，便是位於這一段荷李活道。（圖片由何其銳先生提供）

Old Bailey Street, looking from Hollywood Road, 1981.

⑨　由砵典乍街西望擺花街，約
1906 年。

　　該街道的名稱之前仍為「麟核士
街」，當時是西洋娼妓區。左邊「名煙」
招牌東鄰曾為杏讌樓西菜館。和平後，
這段擺花街有多家女服店及戲服店，不
時會見到粵劇名伶在此選購衣飾。右方
為與威靈頓街交界處。

Lyndhurst Terrace, looking from
Wellington Street, c. 1906.

⑩　在威靈頓街 120 號與嘉咸街交界，
一座位於歷史悠久的唐樓樓下的永和雜
貨店，2001 年。

　　這家老店於淪陷時期曾為配糖站。
曾獲該店的關老闆帶進參觀，見到一座
設有檢驗銀幣真偽坑槽的古董櫃枱。永
和雜貨店的東鄰曾為開業於 1890 年代
的著名正隆包餅店。這座舊樓現仍存在。

Wing Wo Grocery on no. 120
Wellington Street, 2001.

由皇后大道中望向卑利街，約 1938 年。

這條關於 1840 年代的登山道，是以當時英國外交大臣卑利
(Sir Robert Peel) 命名。由二十世紀初起，此街為一市集式街道，
直到現時亦維持此風格。左方為與皇后大道中 136 號交界、於
1927 年開業的蓮香茶室（蓮香樓）。

Peel Street, looking from Queen's Road Central, c. 1938. The first
generation Lin Heung Teahouse is on the left.

⑫ **1959 年，由士他花利街東望威靈頓街。**

左方位於 99 號的唐樓現仍存在。當時著名跌打醫師夏漢雄於二樓開診，其哲嗣為夏國璋。右方為涼茶蔗汁店透心涼，東鄰是大光明蔴雀學校。與卑利街交界的是泰昌大押。夏漢雄的招牌右下方是仍有騎樓的永和雜貨店。

Wellington Street, looking east from Staveley Street, c. 1959. Various shops are situated on the street.

⑬ **由卑利街上望荷李活道，2005 年。**

右方為開業於 1910 年代的振隆米舖，左鄰是戰後（1948 年）開張的公利竹蔗水店，其門面裝潢可用「60 年不變」來形容。其左方的卑利街，亦曾有一靠牆涼茶檔，此外亦有三檔承接寫招牌大字和代寫書信者。

Sugar cane juice shop and grocery on Hollywood Road, 2005.

 由伊利近街下望俗稱「師姑街」的士丹頓街，2004 年農曆中秋期間。

懸掛花牌的街道是卑利街，花牌的右下方是街旁的大伯公廟。這一帶現時已是「全盤西化」的「蘇豪區」(SOHO, South of Hollywood Road)。

Festival decoration of a road-side temple located at the junction of Peel Street and Staunton Streets (SOHO area), 2004.

⑮ 由百子里口東望結志街，2001 年。

　　老牌的浩棧地產現仍營業。位於左方的整列樓宇已被拆卸，以興建新型住宅大廈，與及肉類果菜市場。

Gage Street, looking east from Pak Tsz Lane, 2001.

 結志街 52 號與鴨巴甸街（右）交界的一間「旵冗」麵店，2008 年。

這座於 1970 年代中重建落成的樓宇，之前舊樓的二樓為 1901 年革命志士楊衢雲被暗殺之處。

Corner noodles shop, at the corner of Gage Street and Aberdeen Street, 2008.

 中環鴨巴甸街，約 1950 年。

　　左方為由中醫曾老安開設，兼賣涼茶的曾安堂藥行。其對上結志街 52 號的電髮廳所在樓宇二樓，為楊衢雲被殺之處。其旁靠牆的大興雜貨檔，曾出售每隻 4 毫，用生油作燃料的鐵船仔。鐵船仔可在一面盆的水面上繞圈行駛，為當時孩童們至愛玩具。

　　Aberdeen Street, c. 1950. Gage Street is in the middle left.

18 鴨巴甸街與威靈頓街（橫互）交界，
約 1935 年。

　　煤氣燈左方的一品陞菜館所在現為
蓮香茶室。

Aberdeen Street, looking from
Queen's Road Central, c. 1935. The house
behind the street lamp is where the
nowaday's Li Heung Teahouse located.

約 1925 年的歌賦街，橫亘的是鴨巴甸街。

　　正中為位於鴨巴甸街 6 號的俊和押。右端花檔後曾有一間楊耀記，孫中山先生曾在此會見革命同志。這一帶的三數座舊樓於 1970 年代初改建為中山樓。當時，歌賦街已有包括石華堂等若干間印務館。到了和平後，這裏演變為知名的印務和報業街。位於 21 號石華堂的所在，附近為現時的九記牛腩店。

Aberdeen Street and Gough Street, c. 1925.

20 由荷李活道下望俗稱「大石級」的善慶街，約 1923 年。

　　善慶街早期名為善慶里，亦曾為疫區。正中位於歌賦街的唐樓上，開設了陶英英文學校及文耀漢文學校。陶英的校長伍榮樞曾於 1919 年 6 月 6 日「五四運動」之後，號召學生手持書有「國貨」字樣的雨傘，在街上結隊聯行而被當局檢控。學校左端與城隍街交界處為循環日報社。善慶街右方為大光日報總編輯所，而新聞記者俱樂部亦於 1929 年設於左方 9 號樓宇的三樓。

Shin Hing Street, looking from Hollywood Road, c. 1923.　Gough Street is at the back.

介乎鴨巴甸街（左）以及右端荷李活道、於 1889 年落成的第二代中央書院，約 1900 年。

第一代中央書院於 1862 年在歌賦街與城隍街交界落成，其對面之處於 1874 年為循環日報社。中央書院新校址原為寮屋區，書院曾易名為維多利亞書院，到了 1894 年定名為皇仁書院。校舍於淪陷時被拆毀，和平後亦曾被用作寮屋區，1951 年建成已婚警察宿舍，即現在的元創坊（PMQ）。新皇仁書院同年在銅鑼灣落成。

Queen's College, situated between Hollywood Road and Aberdeen Street (left), c. 1900.

由鴨巴甸街西望「卅間」的士丹頓街，2006 年農曆七月盂蘭勝會期間。

拍攝時正舉行法事。右方是現為元創坊（PMQ）的已婚警察宿舍。「卅間」的名稱，源於早期有一富商在這條街一口氣購入 30 幢樓宇而廣為流傳。

Staunton Street, looking from Aberdeen Street, during the Hungry Ghost Festival, 2006.

 位於城隍街（左）與士丹頓街交界的皇仁書院，約 1905 年。

　　右方位於必列啫士街唐樓當中的 2 號，曾為美國公理會佈道所，孫中山先生曾寄居於此並接受基督教洗禮。淪陷期間這一帶被戰火摧毀，成為「卅間廢墟」。皇仁書院原址於 1951 年建成警察宿舍，現為元創坊（PMQ）。右方唐樓的遺址於 1953 年建成街市。該街市由 2012 年起被改建為香港新聞博覽館，於 2018 年 12 月 5 日開幕。

Rear part of the Queen's College, situated between Shing Wong Street (left) and Staunton Street, c. 1905.

 由必列啫士街上望城隍街，約 1935 年。

正中可見堅道的住宅及山頂的盧吉道。榮興水電的招牌背後是寶華台。右方的唐樓於淪陷時毀於戰火，所在現為香港新聞博覽館。其背後為永利街。

Shing Wong Street, looking from Staunton Street, c. 1935. Caine Road is at the back, and Wing Lee Street is on the middle right.

25 位於必列啫士街與城隍街交界，落成
於 1953 年的必列啫士街街市，2002 年。

街市現已變身為香港新聞博覽館。

Bridges Street Market, 2002. The
Market has been turned into the Hong Kong
News-Expo in December 2018.

26 由荷李活道上望城隍街，1977 年。

上海商務印書館的香港支店，於
1913 年 10 月 25 日在這一帶的荷李活道
82 號（現荷李活華庭所在）開幕試業。正
中可見現為元創坊（PMQ）的警察宿舍。
左方的古玩店前身，為曾是把筵席「送上
門」到港督府之「包辦館」咸記，當時十
分「威水」。

Shing Wong Street and the Police
Married Quarters, looking from Hollywood
Road, 1977.

27 位於歌賦街尾端,被稱為「百步梯」的石級路段中間,伸延至樓梯街之弓絃巷,1976年。

　　弓絃巷的俗名為「竹樹坡」,其上有若干間製紙盒、機器及藥材磨粉的店舖,當中以稱為「落爐舖」的回收舊金銀首飾店最多。1970年代後期,介乎城隍街與禧利街的一段弓絃巷連同樓宇全被夷平。包括右上方荷李活道的唐樓,於2003年建成住宅屋苑荷李活華庭。

Old houses on Circular Pathway, Sheung Wan, 1976. The area is where the nowaday's Hollywood Terrace located.

28 1977年的荷李活道。

　　右方多座背向弓絃巷的百年樓宇正中,有一間位於139號的就昌傢俬店。對面為於此圖外的華僑日報社。左中部位於文武廟旁的古董店現仍存在。

Old houses on no. 137 to 145 of Hollywood Road, 1977.

27 | 28

 由水池巷東望荷李活道，1977 年。

右中部為樓梯街及文武廟，廟旁的學校大樓現仍存在。學校東端的龐大建築物為華僑日報社。

Man Mo Temple near Hollywood Road, 1977. The office of *Wah Kiu Yat Po* is situated in the building in the middle.

1894 年 5 月，在上環太平山區爆發疫症，造成多人死亡。

　　圖中可見英軍及醫護人員在該區進行清潔和清毒工作。這區的樓宇大部分稍後均被清拆。當年，這一帶亦是第一代華人妓寨區的「太平山娼院區」。

A plague-ridden street in Tai Ping Shan area, Sheung Wan, May 1894.

由堅道下望樓梯街，約 1925 年。

右方與堅道 147 號的地段，於 1951 年為崇基學院。左中部為儒林台及老沙路街，其下端的樓宇曾為美華會、公理堂及安懷女學校。有長煙囪的建築是落成於 1918 年的第二代青年會。正中偏右是文武廟廣場，其背後是面向摩羅上街的弓絃巷。

Ladder Street, looking from Caine Road, c. 1925. The building with long chimney in the middle is the YMCA building (second generation).

 必列啫士街青年會，1981 年。

此幢於 1918 年在疫區落成的樓宇，內設有室內泳池及跑道，為當時始創。樓梯街旁的威靈頓英文書院，現為東華醫院住宅屋苑東盛台所在。青年會的所在於疫症發生前名為「左時里西」。

The YMCA building on Bridges Street, 1981.

33 由荷李活道下望西街，1928 年。

　　可見包括富貴全、慶樂山房、寶萬年等多家為粵劇、宴會和喜慶場合配樂助興的大小「八音館」，以及福壽來戲班。此外，還有一省港改良配景手托戲（木偶戲）班。下端與摩羅下街交界的地方則有一間永昌燈籠店。此街的上端亦有音樂儀仗店卉恒興。大部分西街與及摩羅下街於 1970 年代後期開始重建為可通車的樂古道。

Sai Street, where numerous Chinese opera and music offices established, looking from Hollywood Road, 1928.

34　約 1985 年，太平山街接近磅巷的觀音堂。

其右方為落成於 1902 年 5 月的新孖廟，當時，廟內供奉天后、包公、黃大仙、侯王、觀音及綏靖伯等神祇。1990 年代，這一帶大部分的廟宇被拆卸，改建為住宅大廈。

Koon Yum Temple and the temple of various Gods (right) on Tai Ping Shan Street, Sheung Wan, c. 1985.

35　磅巷與太平山街交界，約 1988 年。

高台上為新孖廟、水月宮及觀音廟，部分包括濟公等神祇是由位於灣仔因興建胡忠大廈而清拆之迪龍里遷至此者。這一帶尤其是被稱為「百姓廟」的廣福義祠，之前是農曆驚蟄「打小人」勝地。1960 年代，此勝地遷至銅鑼灣堅拿道兩端。

Temple of various Gods above the terrace between Pound Lane and Tai Ping Shan Street (left), c. 1988.

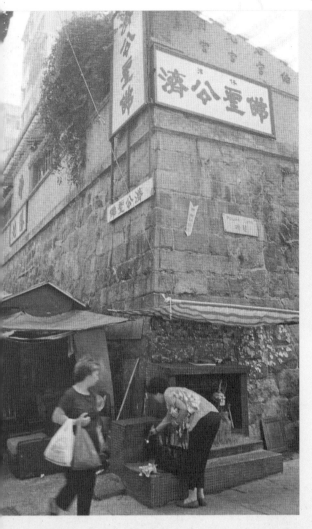

(36) 設於荷李活道與差館上街之間，接近磅巷的一條無名石級道上的老牌鞋檔，2003 年。

自和平後起，這一帶包括東街、西街、水巷、水池巷以至樓梯街，其上有不少鞋檔、攝影檔、洋服恤衫檔及理髮檔等，服務普羅街坊市民。此外，亦有雲吞、魚蛋粉及粥麵檔，當中以吳源記粥麵較著名。70 年代，吳源記發展為一家三層高酒家。

A shoe stall located at a step alley between Hollywood Road and Upper Station Street, 2003.

35 | 36

西區考察遊

Route 4

Tour on Western District

前言

步行的起點是「南北行街」(文咸西街),即「三角碼頭」以西的碼頭區,包括米行雲集和有多座碼頭的干諾道西、由鹹魚欄演變為海味街的德輔道西、西營盤「中心點」的正街及兩旁的街道。新舊七號差館及周遭的香港大學、貨倉和工廠。印象最深刻的是設於干諾道西,以及旁邊的朝光街、西邊街及正街,那道於黃昏起關閉的保安街閘,充滿森嚴肅殺的氣氛。

使人感興趣的,是由山道、皇后大道西和德輔道西等街道構成,位於屈地街煤氣廠以西的「塘西風月區」,雖然已消失了 80 多年,但在此「城開不夜、紙醉金迷」煙花之地中的「紅牌阿姑」倩影,仍縈繞在不少人之腦際。

1870 年代,在西環卑路乍灣填海而獲致的堅尼地城,早期為貨倉、工廠、碼頭和船廠區,最龐大者是創設於 1885 年的香港蔴纜廠,於 1960 年代中改建為聯邦新樓住宅羣。

當時,西環仍頗為荒涼,市民往西環主要是到域多利道的兩座泳場。近年,港鐵開通至西環,該區旋即有翻天覆地的變化。

Introduction

The tour takes off at "Nam Pak Hong Street" (Bonham Strand West) Triangular Pier (or Wing Lok Street Wharf) exploring the pier along Praya Kennedy Town. In earlier times, there were many piers serving rice importing firms established along Connaught Road West. The traditional salted fish market has transformed itself into the present-day dried seafood hub. The focus is now centred around Centre Street, plus the environs of the University of Hong Kong and the many side-streets, lanes and alley-ways that litter the area, providing spaces for shops, store-houses, godowns and small factories. The most intense memory comes from the recollection of the erection of security gates which were lowered at dusk across the central parts of Connaught Road West, Chiu Kwong Street, Western Street and Centre Street. These gates prevented unauthorized vehicular access and conjured up a deep sense of tense security and foreboding.

Of deeper interest to the itinerant is the Shek Tong Tsui brothel area which covered the environs of Hill Road, the section of Queen's Road West next to the coal gas tanks on Whitty Street and part of Des Voeux Road West. Although 80 years or more has elapsed after prostitution was banned in 1935, sweet memories still linger in the minds of revellers past who relished the delights of "the City that never sleeps". Eat, drink and make merry for tomorrow may tarry. The services provided by top-notch ladies of the night and others must have left an indelible impression in the minds of many contended clients.

In the 1870's, the reclamation of Belcher Bay area provided new land (Kennedy Town) for the construction and provision of godowns, factories, piers and small ship repair yards. A rather large-scale rope making works was set up in 1885 along Forbes Street between Davis Street and Smithfield, and since the 1960's this area has phoenixed into a vast residential complex, the Luen Bong Mansion.

In the early 20th century, Western district was a quite desolate and out-of-the way area. Nonetheless, quite a few people often went there to patronise the several swimming sheds along a stretch of Victoria Road. Only one now remains, the Sai Wan. The extension of the MTR Island line to Kennedy Town has transformed the area into a vibrant and prosperous part of wonderful Hong Kong.

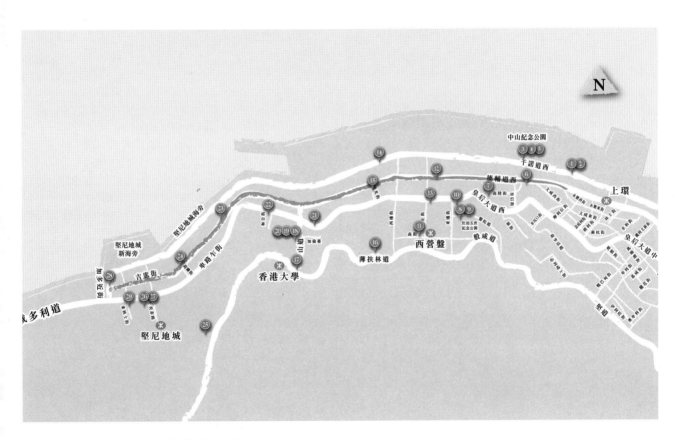

Please scan the below QR code for English map.

位於三角碼頭西端，西營盤干諾道西的一座簡陋碼頭，約 1925 年。

前方有一名正在「擔泥」的客家婦女。車頂有雙妹化粧品廣告之汽車背後，可見一艘大洋船的煙囪。

A pier on Connaught Road West, Sai Ying Pun, c. 1925.

1928 年西營盤干諾道西。一名肩負重擔、由貨艇走過狹長跳板登岸的「碼頭咕哩」(搬運工人)。

他手中持有以竹枝製成，用來計算「力金」(工資) 的「籌」。坐在旁邊者是負責「派籌」的婦人。

A loading coolie on Connaught Road West, Sai Ying Pun, 1928.

約 1960 年的西營盤海旁干諾道西。

右中部可見於 1958 年由國家醫院改建而成的西營盤賽馬會診所。其前方的舊樓為包括英源、茂益隆、廣承興、義興祥及義和隆等多家入口及批發的米行。前方泊有一艘滿載柴束的帆船。

The seafront on Connaught Road West, Sai Ying Pun, c. 1960.

1	2
3	

 1985 年的干諾道西。

　　正中為 58 號的入口米商義和隆。右方與皇后街交界的是潮州火鍋店潮江號。80 年代的皇后街上，有多家食店和大牌檔，入夜後有大量食客，包括有駕名車者由各方湧至。（圖片由陳創楚先生提供）

Rice dealers and Chiu Chow restaurant on Connaught Road West, 1985.

⑤ 約 1960 年的干諾道西。潮退時市民在海上用「罩厘」淘沙「摸蜆」。

　　可見兩艘搭架登峰狹長跳板的貨艇。背後是供來往深水埗及南丫島小輪停泊的威利蔴街碼頭。

People searching for shell fish of the outgoing tide. Connaught Road West near the Sham Shui Po and Lamma Island Ferry Pier, c. 1960.

⑥ 1989 年 11 月，英國皇儲查理斯王子（Prince Charles）訪港，參觀在德輔道西 50 號鹹魚欄區一家海味店。

Prince Charles of the United Kingdom visiting a dry seafrood shop at Sai Ying Pun, 1989.

⑦ 約 2010 年農曆八月中秋節前，位於西營盤近李陞街的兩間紙料紮作店，店前展示各種花燈。

Mid Autumn Festival lantern shops on Queen's Road West, Sai Ying Pun, 2010.

 位於東邊街與醫院道之間，政府國家醫院前的花園，約 1915 年。

左後方為於 1892 年落成的護士宿舍，後於 1939 年改作精神病院。現為社區綜合大樓。1936 年，該公園開始改建成為英皇佐治五世公園，於 1954 年才告落成。

Government Civil Hospital Quarters and garden, Sai Ying Pun, c. 1915.

 由醫院道下望東邊街，約 1932 年。

左方為第一街。右方醫院道旁的唐樓，有兩間水草批發及零售店。當時的水草主要用作綁扎餸菜魚肉及日用品者。中部可見德輔道西的電車。

Eastern Street, looking down from Hospital Road, c. 1932.

⑩ 位於皇后大道近西湖里的王老吉涼茶
店，2003年。

西湖里後方正進行地下鐵路工程。

A Chinese herb tea shop, Wang Lo Kut
on Queen's Road West, 2003.

8	9
	10

Street H.K.

HONGKONG—PART OF QUEEN'S ROA

由高街下望正街，約 1925 年。

中左部有於 1864 年建成的第一代西營盤街市，稍後在右方的第二街、第三街之間加建另一座新型街市。正中海旁有一座稱為「渣甸橋」的怡和碼頭。每逢農曆中元節，該區坊眾會在此舉辦「渣甸橋盂蘭勝會」，與「三角碼頭」坊眾所舉辦的勝會互相輝映。

Centre Street, looking down from High Street, c. 1925.

由正街東望德輔道西，約 1920 年。

兩旁有多家鹹魚、鹹蛋及海味店，故該區被稱為「鹹魚欄」。鹹魚欄原設於內地陳村，1880 年代的一場颶風，導致捕曬鹹魚的漁船灣泊於西營盤銷售，後因生意頗佳由內地移至此。現時，西營盤一帶已由鹹魚欄變身為海味街。

The "salty fish market" on Des Voeux Road West, the nowaday's "dry seafood market", looking east from Centre Street, c. 1920.

1989 年的皇后大道西，中間為正街。

左方為老牌的多男茶樓，於 1996 年結業時成為傳媒焦點。右方滙豐銀行所在的八達大廈前身為於 1930 年代開業的正心茶樓。

Dor Nam, a famous teahouse, situated between Queen's Road West and Centre Street, 1989.

```
11
12 | 13
```

 約 1910 年的西營盤海旁。

左方有兩座金字塔屋頂的建築是九龍倉，其前方為渣甸橋（碼頭）。大洋船背後為均益貨倉和招商局貨倉及右方碼頭。尖塔所在的聖彼得教堂和右方的海員之家，於 1955 年同被改建為新七號警署。右方兩座金字塔屋頂的建築亦為均益貨倉。這一帶的工廠、貨倉還有煤氣廠，於 1950 年代起陸續被改建為商住樓宇。

Godowns and factories at the seafront of Connaught Road West, between Western Street and Water Street, c. 1910.

Des Veoux Road and Electric Car, Sailor's Home and St. Peter's Church, Hongkong.

 由朝光街東望德輔道西,約 1908 年。

　　煤氣燈旁是招商局貨倉,東鄰數座金字塔屋頂的是均益貨倉。右中部為聖彼得教堂的尖塔,而右方為僅露出三角屋頂的海員之家 (些那堪,Sailor's Home)。兩者於 1955 年被改建為新七號警署。

Des Voeux Road West, c. 1908. The Sailors' Home and Saint Peter's Church were re-built into the new Western Police Station in 1955.

於薄扶林道交界、1912 年重建落成的第二代七號差館（西區警署），約 1950 年。

1955 年，警署遷往德輔道西與西邊街交界的地段後，舊警署被改建為西區裁判署。

Western Police Station (second generation) situated on Pokfulam Road, c. 1950.

約 **1925** 年的石塘咀區。

可見橫亙於薄扶林道上的香港大學解剖學館。前方為山道正中的大水坑，而山道與皇后大道西和德輔道西一帶之風月區，因而亦被稱為「新水坑口」及「水塘口」。1926 年，山道及水坑被大雨沖毀，稍後水坑被蓋平變為暗渠，發展成可行車的道路。

The nullah on Hill Road, c. 1925. The anatomy building of the University of Hong Kong is at the back.

18
19
20

18 由 遇 安 台 及 南 里 下 望 山 道，約 1918 年。

可 見 位 於 山 道 正 中 的 明 渠 水 坑。右 方 為 共 和 酒 樓（前 身 是 洞 天 酒 家），1927 年 改 建 為 第 二 代 金 陵 酒 家。皇 后 大 道 西 另 一 端 金 字 塔 屋 頂 的 建 築 是 太 湖 酒 家。左 鄰 是 妓 寨「四 大 天 王」：倚 紅、詠 樂、賽 花 及 歡 得（現 為 長 發 大 廈）；左 鄰 是 香 江 酒 樓（現 為 太 平 洋 廣 場）。電 車 站 右 方 是 陶 園 酒 家，現 為 香 港 商 業 中 心。

The Chinese restaurants and brothels on Hill Road and Queen's Road West, looking down from South Lane, c. 1918.

19 1926 年 7 月 17 日 雨 災 後 的 石 塘 咀 山 道。

可 見 被 大 水 沖 毀 的 明 渠。背 後 為 加 倫 臺、遇 安 台 及 南 里 一 帶 的 樓 宇。

Hill Road of Shek Tong Tsui, after a rainstorm on 17 July, 1926.

20 1926 年雨災後的山道，當時這段路中的明渠已被蓋平。

左方依次為香江酒樓、妓寨「四大天王」：依次為歡得、賽花、詠樂及倚紅，和太湖酒家。最高者為興建中的金陵酒家。正中為位於遇安台（後併入南里）與南里之間的聯陞酒店。聯陞的右旁是數座妓寨及頤和酒家。最右者是第一代金陵酒家，稍後改為廣州酒家。

The Chinese reataurants and brothels on Hill Road and South Lane, after a rainstorm in 1926.

138

 1934 年 5 月 14 日，石塘咀煤氣廠之煤氣鼓（儲藏庫）發生爆炸。

　　旁邊的皇后大道西、加倫臺及晉成街（現已消失）共幾十座樓宇被焚，數十人死傷。圖中為由山道東望皇后大道西，正中現為聖類斯中學所在。左右兩方仍有若干家酒樓和妓院。救火車的右方是晉成街。

Explosion of a gas factory situated between Whitty Street and Queen's Road West, on 14 May 1934.

22 由和合街東望皇后大道西，1969 年。

金豪酒樓（現為麥當勞餐廳）所在前身為金陵酒家。正中的西環大樓前身為曾爆炸的煤氣鼓。山道右邊的米店和新生池浴室所在，現時為今旅酒店。（圖片由麥勵濃先生提供）

Queen's Road West, Shek Tong Tsui, looking east from Wo Hop Street, 1969.

23 1906 年 9 月 18 日，一場致命颶風襲港後的石塘咀與西環交界的堅彌地城海旁。

可見數輛被吹至出軌及損毀的電車。左方一輛的背後是皇后大道西。圖中那些被稱為「石騎樓」的樓宇，大部分為低級廉價妓院。

Low grade brothels on praya of Kennedy Town, after a tyhoon attack on 18 September, 1906.

 1987 年，由荷蘭街東望堅彌地城海旁。

　　圖中的富華貨倉及和益貨倉，稍後被改建為住宅大廈。貨車背後為西祥街。旁邊南雄大廈東鄰的
呂興合冷房貨倉，現為中遠酒店所在。（圖片由陳創楚先生提供）

Cold storage and godowns on praya of Kennedy Town, looking east from Holland Street, 1987.

25 落成於 1884 年的西環青蓮臺魯班先師廟，2005 年。

擁有這一帶物業的李姓大業主，用青蓮太白、伏羲上人來為物業所在的街道命名，如青蓮臺、義皇臺等。1915 年，這一帶開設了一間李苑太白樓及遊樂場，所在現為太白臺。

Lo Pan Temple on Ching Lin Terrace, 2005.

26 1885 年，在西環卑路乍街 102 號，與士美菲路交界創立的香港蔴纜廠內部，約 1900 年。

1880 年代中，被稱為「垃圾灣」的卑路乍灣填海工程完成，西環旋即成為華人新居住區，香港蔴纜廠亦同時落成。廠房於 1960 年代中被拆卸，改建為住宅樓宇聯邦新樓。附近「牛房」對上的山邊及墓葬地段，於兩、三年後亦興建了觀龍樓大型公共屋邨。

The inner part of the Hong Kong Rope Factory, situated at the junction of Belcher's Street and the Smithfield, Kennedy Town, c. 1900.

Kennedy Town

西環卑路乍街與士美菲路交界的香港蔴纜廠景致，約 1905 年。

The scenery of the Hong Kong Rope Factory, Kennedy Town, c. 1905.

約 1905 年的堅尼地城，由加多近街東望遮打街 (1909 年易名為吉席街)。

這一帶包括堅彌地城新海旁的地段，是於 1870 年代中開始進行的填海所獲致的。之前的舊海旁是卑路乍街。由於是次堅尼地城填海，以及 1889 年起的中西區填海，均由遮打爵士 (Sir Catchick Paul Chater) 主催，故該條街道被命名為遮打街。1909 年，易名為吉席街 (「吉席」(Catchick) 是遮打爵士的中間名字)。圖中可見於 1904 年起通車之電車路軌，兩旁可見民居及貨倉。

Chater Street (renamed as to Catchick Street in 1909) in Kennedy Town, looking east from Cadogan Street, c. 1905.

位於西環卑路乍街 (右) 及爹核士街 (左) 交界的老牌陳李濟藥廠，1992 年。

和平後，這間藥廠、其對面的香港蔴纜廠 (現為聯邦新樓)，還有現已改為頤養院的消防局，於 1950 年代，在頗為荒涼的西環是較引人注目的地標。

A Chinese medicine factory located between Belcher's Street (right) and Davis Street (left), Kennedy Town.

路線五

金鐘及灣仔懷舊遊

Route 5

Nostaglic Tour on Admiralty and
Wan Chai District

前言

　　長久以來，「下環」及灣仔的起點，為花園道及美利道起以東的地段。位於這地段的幹道為皇后大道東，約1970年易名為金鐘道。

　　金鐘道兩旁，自1845年起闢建了三座軍營及一座海軍船塢，到了1958年，此軍事地帶交回港府作民用，以開闢道路和社會設施，及作商業發展，當中著名軍營地標美利樓，亦於1990年改建成中銀大廈。其他地標還有樂禮大樓的「金鐘」，亦有起源於一家日本古物店的「大佛口」。

　　經過始於1841年、1921年、1951年及1963年的四次大規模填海，灣仔及銅鑼灣區變化翻天覆地，海岸線亦由皇后大道東、莊士敦道連同軒尼詩道、告士打道，依次伸延至現時的博覽道、會議道及鴻興道等。

　　其中，於1963年開展在告士打道進行的填海工程完成後，在新填地上築建了海底隧道及會議展覽中心，旋即使灣仔成為足以與中環分庭抗禮的商貿重鎮。

　　這主題的行程，分為四條路線：

　　第一條由遮打花園出發，經過原來的美利軍營、海軍船塢、「死亡彎角」旁的域多利軍營，內有「金鐘大樓」的威靈頓軍營。然後，探索昔日軍器廠、大佛洋行、防空洞的「大佛口」地段，以及其旁之法國教會、第一代發電廠以及安樂水房所在的「杉排」。然後，是大王廟及其對開填海地段的船廠、機器廠、碼頭和貨倉，還有洋娼區的春園街和三板街。

　　十多年前，多在大王西街一家現已結業的魚蛋粉麵店歇腳，品嚐美味的食品。後來則改為在春園街與三板街之間一小公園小休，出席者可往對面的金鳳餐室選購凍啡、奶茶、雞批或菠蘿油，大快朵頤。

　　然後，徒步經舊灣仔三號警署遺跡和郵政局、新舊街市和石水渠街的「藍屋」，參觀隆安街的玉虛宮。最後，在旁邊的花園了解該一帶的發展，以及醫院山和摩理臣山的變遷。不時，承蒙聖雅各福群會分派予每位出席者若干份，當中亦有介紹香港舊貌的長者刊物《松柏之聲》。行程在此解散，若意猶未盡，可前往附近之玩具街（太原街）、喜帖街（利東街）及巴士街的前「動漫基地」（現稱茂蘿街七號）等景點瀏覽。

　　第二條路線由「藍屋」起步，經原灣仔峽道的皇后大道東，介紹醫院山（現律敦治醫院所在）和摩理臣山（現鄧肇堅醫院所在）。在錫克教廟前可了解司徒拔道等往半山及南區道路的開闢過程。

之後，經過戰前工展會舉辦地點伊利沙伯體育館，並在此遙望馬場及黃泥涌道，了解馬場的演進和附近遊樂場、昔日黃泥涌村的變遷，和歷年禮頓山上的房屋。

過了摩理臣山道，在禮頓道和堅拿道交界，了解這區若干條街道名稱的變更，這一帶糖廠、電車廠、南洋兄弟煙草公司，以及早期的運河（堅拿，canal）與若干座橋樑的關係。

隨後，轉入軒尼詩道「打小人」的熱點，過了波斯富街，了解渣甸山（利園山）及早期渣甸洋行（怡和洋行）的貨倉、糖廠和紡織廠，與及法國聖保祿醫院及學校，還有 1860 年代的鑄錢局。在中央圖書館旁，造訪大坑村、蓮花宮，以及其背後的浣紗塘、大坑道、虎豹別墅，又可了解渣甸山和這一帶高尚住宅的發展歷程。之後，可各自在大坑區的食肆休憩及享受美食。

第三條路線由「大佛口」軒尼詩道起步，了解 1921 年開始的灣仔填海起點、新舊軍器廠街、軍器廠，以及麗的呼聲電台和電視台。

然後，步入莊士敦道，經過往日的分域機器廠，由填海而獲致的「市肺」修頓球場；附近的年宵市場和包括雙喜、龍鳳（後來的龍門）、英京等茶樓和酒家；包括麗都、金城（1951-1957）、東城、香港、東方等戲院，之後是二號差館舊址和早期這一帶的船廠及碼頭。

由修頓球場前往軒尼詩道，了解早期的特色店舖，再步入駱克道，探索淪陷時期的「日本人聚樂街」，以及和平後之「麗絲黃的世界」酒吧區。在三十年代「新海旁」的告士打道，了解著名的建築如酒店、煙廠、新二號差館、怡和的貨倉及午炮等，還可了解吉列島（奇力島）的演變、紅隧的興建，以及工展會場地所在的建築物和附近的香港會議展覽中心。

最後，在維多利亞公園了解銅鑼灣及高士威道的名稱、1883 年的第一座避風塘和維園的興建，以及年宵花市的前世今生。

第四條路線起步點於灣仔莊士敦道，途經汕頭街、利東街、太原街、茂羅街、史釗域道、堅拿道，至告士打道海旁。

Introduction

From time immemorial "Ha Wan", literally had its boundaries from Garden Road and Murray Road to the east. The main trunk road traversing this area was initially known as "Queen Road East" and in around 1970, it was renamed as "Queensway".

As far back as 1845, the "Queensway" area was home to three military barracks and a naval dockyard. It was not until 1958 that the military complex was handed over to the local government for municipal purposes, e.g. building of new road, establishing community facilities and for commercial developments. The majestic Murray House was dismantled (later reassembled piece by piece in Stanley). The Bank of China Tower soon rose from the empty site in 1990. Other notable landmarks included the former Rodney House (at present-day Harcourt Garden) and a Japanese run Daibutsu curio shop located at the junction of Arsenal Street and Queen's Road East. The junction gradually came to be known as "Dai Fut (Daibutsu) Hau".

After the vast reclamation schemes initiated in the years 1841, 1921, 1951 and 1963, the city scape of Wan Chai and Causeway Bay changed beyond all recognition with all the "old" coastlines as indicated by Queen's Road East, Johnston Road, Hennessy Road and Gloucester Road having been advanced northwards and new thoroughfares created, such as Expo Drive, Convention Avenue and Hung Hing Road.

The completion of the reclamation scheme initiated in 1963 along Gloucester Road created new land for the building of the Cross Harbour Tunnel and the Hong Kong Convention and Exhibition Centre. Hence, Wanchai rose in importance and became comparable to Central as a thriving commercial hot spot.

There are four separate trails to cover for this themed tour.

The first route starts at Chater Garden, then tread past the former sites of Murray Parade Ground and Barracks, the naval dockyard and the infamous "death bend" (this refers to the bottleneck section of Queen's Road East. The bend in the road was 90 degrees leading to frequent occurrences of vehicular accidents), the vast Victoria Barracks which were home to the Wellington Barracks. The itinerant then engages in "exploring" the old Arsenal Street, Daibutsu, nearby bomb shelters and then proceed to Saint

Francis Street and Saint Francis yard which were the sites of a cemetery and later the site of Hong Kong's first electric power plant. Then try to look for the remnants of the Connaught aerated soft drinks and beverages company. Visitors then visit the Tai Wong Temple, Ship Street and Schooner Street and look for signs of any existing small machine shops / factories and possible locations of former piers and godowns. The more interesting discovery is to find out as much as possible about the tales surrounding the former red light district around Spring Garden Lane and Sam Pan Street. The brothels catered mainly to Westerners.

About ten years ago, heritage addicts often rested their tired legs by patronising a now closed snack shop specialising in delicious fishballs with rice noodles. Alternatively, walkers often got a well deserved rest at small garden near Spring Garden Lane and Sam Pan Street to catch their breath and became more energised for the next part of the tour. One's hunger can be satisfied by visiting the popular Kam Fung Cha Chaan Teng to savour its famous iced coffee, milk tea, chicken pie or pineapple bun.

After feeling refreshed, visitors may endeavour to reach for the original sites of the number three police station, the old Post Office, the new and former Wanchai Market, the famous Blue House Cluster on Stone Nullah Lane. Then venture to the old Yuk Hui Kung (Jade Void Temple) built in 1863. The Pak Tai statute inside the main hall is about 400 years old. The temple is on Lung On Street. Then, at a nearby garden, visualise the development of the neighbouring area, including Hospital Hill and Morrison Hill. At the nearby Saint James' Settlement there is available the newspaper, *The Voice* with the content of history of Hong Kong.

The trail die-hard seekers, may make their way to visit the well-known Toys Street (Tai Yuen Street), Lee Tung Street (Wedding card Street), Burrows Street and No.7 Mallory Street, which was named the Comix Home Base in the past.

The second route begins at the Blue House Cluster, admiring the location of Hospital Hill (Ruttonjee Hospital), Morrison Hill (present-day Tang Shiu Kin Hospital). Then cool our heels at the Sikh Temple and surmised the development of access road to the Mid-levels and Southern District.

Next, conjecture up visions of the former

site of the Exhibition of Hong Kong Products (present-day Queen Elizabeth Stadium) and carry their minds back to the early days of Wong Nai Chung Village, the Racecourse, Wong Nai Chung Road itself, the various cemeteries and the extensive Leighton Hill apartments.

Treading along Morrison Hill Road, we then arrive at the junction of Leighton Road with Canal Road and as before explore the various side streets, the former Tramway Depot, sugar refineries, the Nanyang Brothers Tobacco Company / Factory and then take a ride on a time machine that brings trekkers back to the days of the building of Bowrington Canal (known in Cantonese as Ngo Keng Kui – Gooseneck Bridge) and attendant constructions.

Next, the itinerants turn into Hennessy Road and come to a spot under the Canal Road flyover where wizened old ladies offer villain beating / hitting services in which personal or presumed enemies are cursed by beating pieces of paper representing the villain with shoe or other implements.

Past Percival Street, again conjure up images or memories and engage in reality checks on Leighton Hill, the former godowns belonging to Jardine Matheson, sugar refineries, the former cotton mill / factory of the present-day Saint Paul's Convent School and the neighbouring Saint Paul's Hospital and a government mint set up in 1860. The trail seekers then made their way towards the Central Public Library, turn into Tai Hang area, visit Lin Fa Temple, Wun Sha Street (which provided a natural clothes washing facility in early times), and search out what remains of the former Tiger Balm Gardens / Haw Par Mansion and admire the development of the various residential complexes in the area. Again, partake of the delights of the multifarious cuisines of the neighbourhood.

The third route starts at the junction of Arsenal Street with Hennessy Road and search for signs and tales about the old Arsenal Street and the location of the former Rediffusion Studios.

We then proceed to Johnston Road, linger around the Fenwick Street precincts, the girlie bar hot-spots looking back to the days of "The World of Suzie Wong". Then browse around the Southorn Playground (built on reclaimed land), the Lunar New Year Fair held there and check out the sites of long vanished Chinese restaurants like Sheung Hei (Double Happiness), Lung Fung (later known as Lung Moon) and former theatres such as Lido, Golden City (1951-1957), the Hong Kong Theatre, the Oriental and East Town Theatre and finally look for signs of the old pier facilities and shipyards.

Exiting Southorn Playground, tread along Hennessy Road where shabby-shop fronts are intertwined with modern chrome and glass fronted businesses. Entering Lockhart Road, we endeavour to locate the haunts of the Japanese during the war era. During the 1930's, there were quite a few majestic buildings erected along Gloucester Road, e.g. the Luk Kwok Hotel, cigarette factory and the Wanchai Police Station. We are able to witness the daily noonday gun ceremony, look across to the Cross Harbour Tunnel complex, the Hong Kong Convention and Exhibition Centre and the area where former Exhibition of Hong Kong Products was held. Visitors can also imagine how Kellet Island would have looked before reclamation joined it to the mainland.

Finally, visitors end up at the Victoria Park, visualising the provision in 1883 of the first typhoon shelter, check upon the nomenclature of Causeway Bay and its environs. The Park itself has for many years been the site of the annual Lunar New Year Fair. We end on a joyful note, having savoured the highlights of Hong Kong's fascinating heritage.

The fourth route commences at Johnston Road, passing through Swatow Street, Lee Tung Avenue, Tai Yuen Street, Mallory Street, Stewart Road, Canal Road and ends at the coast on Gloucester Road.

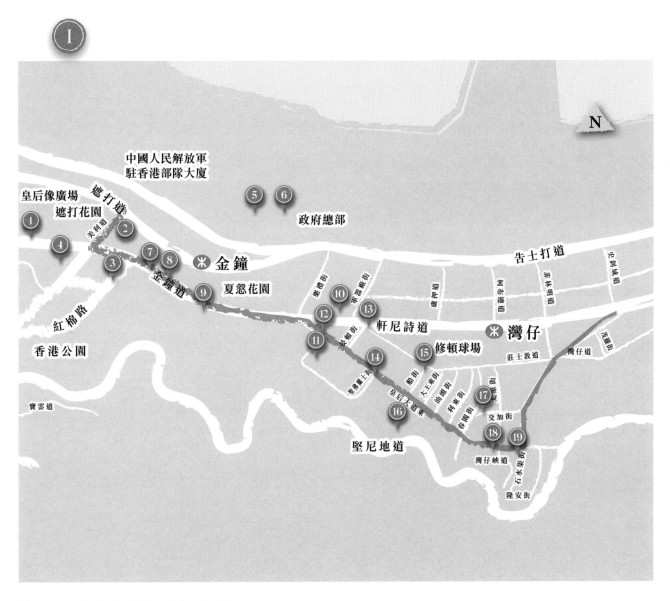

I

皇后像廣場
遮打花園
遮打道
美利道
中國人民解放軍
駐香港部隊大廈
政府總部
告士打道
史釗域道
菲林明道
柯布連道
分域街
軒尼詩道
灣仔
金鐘
金鐘道
夏愨花園
樂禮街
軍器廠街
盧押道
莊士敦道
灣仔道
茂蘿街
紅棉路
香港公園
寶雲道
菲林明士兵房
灣仔道
皇后大道東
船街
大王東街
油街街
利東街
秀華坊
交加街
堅尼地道
石水渠街
灣仔峽道
隆安街

N

①
④
②
③
⑦
⑧
⑨
⑤
⑥
⑩
⑫
⑪
⑬
⑭
⑮
⑯
⑰
⑱
⑲

Please scan the below QR code for English map.

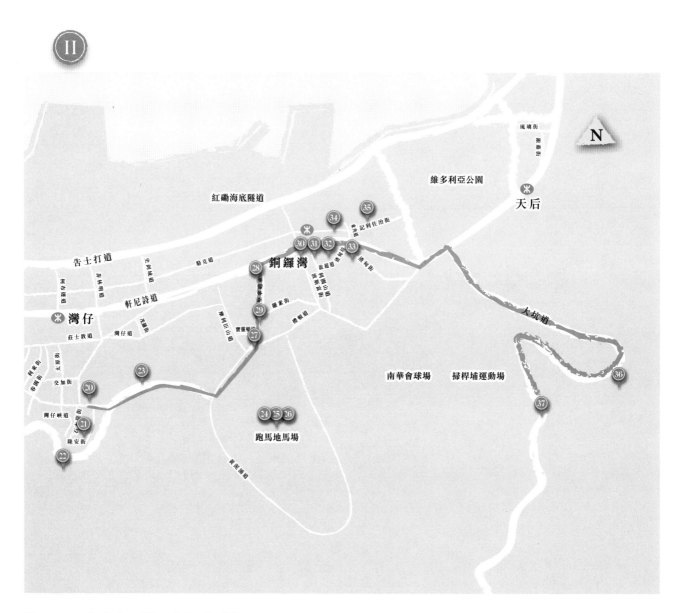

Please scan the below QR code for English map.

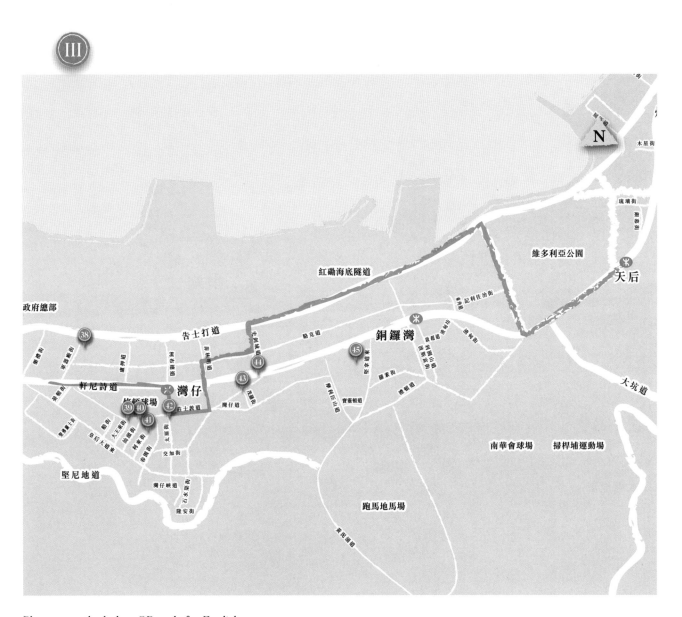

Please scan the below QR code for English map.

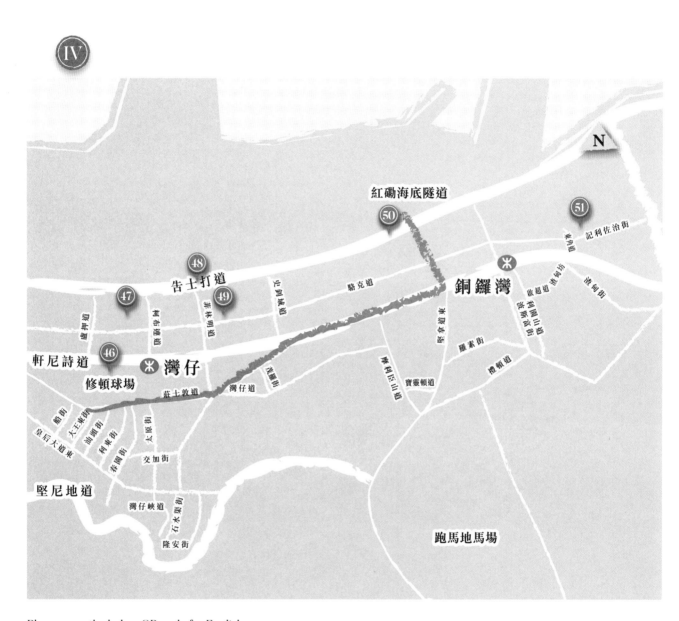

Please scan the below QR code for English map.

① 一輛泊於中環銀行及洋行區的馬車，約 **1900** 年。

　　車伕工作間小睡。當時，包括渣打等銀行，及若干間洋行的司理或「大班」，喜歡於午後乘馬車或小輪前往銅鑼灣東角，或對面的渣甸山，與渣甸（怡和）洋行大班會晤。早期由美利道以東迄至銅鑼灣區的地段名為「下環」。

A horse carriage at bank area, Central District, c. 1900.

 由美利道西望美利操場（左）及木球會（右，現為遮打花園和高等法院），約 1920 年。

電燈桿背後是第二代滙豐銀行的圓屋頂。

Murray Parade Ground (left) and Cricket Ground (right), looking from Murray Road, c. 1920. The City Hall and HSBC Building are at the rear of the tram.

(3) **1953 年 6 月 2 日，慶祝女皇加冕的會景巡遊。**

　　在東華醫院的「觀音坐蓮」花車上，由女明星余群英扮演觀音。花車正經過皇后大道東（金鐘道）美利軍營的樓房。此樓房於 1960 年代被拆卸，1967 年闢成通往半山的紅棉路。

A parade vechicle of the Tung Wah Hospital for the celebration of the coronation of the Queen Elizabeth II is passing through Queen's Road East (Queensway), near the Murray House on June 2, 1953.

 1986 年，位於花園道的希爾頓酒店（現為長江集團中心）。

前方的地盤為剛被拆平、於 1844 年興建的美利樓。地盤後來築建中銀大廈，於 1990 年落成。

The Hilton Hotel on Garden Road, 1986. The Murray House at the front was later rebuilt into the Bank of China Tower, which was completed in 1990.

5 約 1964 年的海軍船塢地段（正中）。

右方美利道的上端為美利樓，其左方正闢建紅棉路。圖左中部分為域多利軍營（現為太古廣場所在）以及威靈頓軍營（現為夏慤花園所在）。正中為夏慤道及添馬海軍船塢（現為政府總部所在）。右下方為皇后碼頭。

Naval dockyard area and Harcourt Road, c. 1964. The Queen's Pier is on the lower right.

6 在原添馬海軍船塢的新填地上，正動工興建政府總部和立法會大樓，約 2009 年。

背景為中國人民解放軍駐香港部隊大廈。

Central Government Offices and Legislative Council Complex are under construction, looking from Tim Mei Avenue, c. 2009.

 海軍船塢和前方的美利樓，約 1925 年。

船塢的右方停泊着白色的「添馬號」軍艦，圖右中部為大佛口的軍器廠。

Naval dockyard and the *Tamar* Warship, at Queensway, c. 1925.

約 1910 年的皇后大道東（金鐘道）。

　　左方海軍船塢的入口處現為力寶中心，右方為美利軍營。正中是被稱為「死亡彎角」的急彎路。背後是域多利軍營（現為太古廣場所在）。該「死亡彎角」於 1970 年代起才逐漸被「拉直」。

The entrance of the naval dockyard on Queen's Road East (Queensway), c. 1910.

1926 年雨災後的皇后大道東（金鐘道）。

右方地段於 19 世紀時為「廣州市場」。貨車背後為蟠龍里的入口牌坊，頂端有蟠龍里的路名石牌。左方是海員俱樂部。這一帶現為高等法院及金鐘道政府合署所在，再隔鄰現為太古廣場。

Queen's Road East after a rainstorm in 1926. The area is where the nowaday's Queensway Government Offices and High Court situated.

 皇后大道東威靈頓軍營樂禮大樓，約 1930 年。

頂端的金色時鐘後來成了「金鐘」名稱的起源。該大樓約於 1970 年重建，新大樓已無「金鐘」，但這段皇后大道東卻同時被易名為「金鐘道」。到了 1990 年代，新樂禮大樓再度被拆卸以開闢夏慤花園，旁邊則留有一條樂禮街。

Rodney Building on Queen's Road East, where the today's Harcourt Garden located, c. 1930.

 皇后大道東的大佛古董行，約 1912 年。

右方域多利軍營的出入口現為正義道。左方是軍器廠。其與大佛古物行之間是第一代軍器廠街，早期電車要經此軍器廠街才轉入「海旁東」（莊士敦道）。長久以來，大佛行為灣仔地標，故這一帶被稱為「大佛口」。右邊的山崗為「大佛山」，位於其左邊海旁東的碼頭為「大佛碼頭」。

Daibutsu Japanese curio shop on Queen's Road East, Wan Chai, c. 1912. The arsenal is on the left.

165 WELINTON BARRACK

Queen's Road East, Hongkong.

12 由麼地爵士（Sir Hormusjee Naorojee Mody）捐款，於 1909 年興建位於海旁東（左）及第一代
軍器廠街（右）的「新水手館」（海軍及海員會所）。

　　會所於 1910 年 6 月 17 日落成，圖片攝於剛落成時。1938 年，此幢建築與及其右鄰的部分樓宇被
拆卸，以闢建軒尼詩道，而軍器廠街亦遷往現時所在。

The just completed Soldiers and Sailor's Home, at the junction of Johnston Road and Arsenal Street (first
generation), 1910.

由金鐘道望軒尼詩道，約 1950 年。

　　前方電車的背後原為「新水手館」所在。右方為由大佛古物行改建的先施保險大樓。左方的原軍營地段後來興建警察宿舍。在軍器廠街旁的是有線電台「麗的呼聲」，於 1960 年代後期改建為熙信大廈。

Hennessy Road, Wan Chai, c. 1950.　The two-storey building at the intersection of new Arsenal Street is the Rediffusion Broadcast Station.

由皇后大道東上望，遭受 1926 年 7 月 17 日大雨沖毀的「杉排」區聖佛蘭士街。

中後方是聖佛蘭士醫院。其左方為秀華坊。右中部是聖嬰里，稍後易名為光明街。光明街以西的日街、月街、星街及電氣街一帶，是 1890 年開始供電之第一代發電廠所在。

St. Francis Street, after a rainstorm on July 17, 1926, looking from Queen's Road East.

15 由船街西望皇后大道東，約 1925 年。

右方可見聯發街口的寰球園西菜館和丸一大藥房。這一帶有位於皇后大道東 98 號地下、東華醫院屬下的集善醫所，在 1929 年演變為東華東院。

Queen's Road East, looking west from Ship Street, c. 1925.

14 | 15

QUEEN'S ROAD EAST

Chinese temple Quee's road East

於香港開埠前建成的洪聖古廟,約 1918 年。

古廟又名「大王廟」、「大王宮」及「石廟」,曾於 1857 年重建。其前方早期為海旁,故廟內有供奉望海觀音。1841 年開展的填海工程完成後,廟前闢有大王東街 (早期名為 Lyall Street) 及大王西街。

Hung Shing Temple on Queen's Road East, Wan Chai, c. 1918.

由交加街北望春園街,約 1925 年。

這一帶與及附近的三板街,為西洋及日本妓寨區,可見一些包括外國水兵等尋芳客。為吸引「食回頭草」的嫖客,街號門牌寫得特大,故被稱為「大冧巴」(big number) 妓寨區。自 1933 年起,這一帶率先禁娼,不少「無地自容」的外籍妓女,改在修頓球場附近一帶拉客。

The foreign and Japanese brothel area on Spring Garden Lane, Wan Chai, c. 1925.

於 1915 年開始營業的灣仔郵政分局,1985 年。

這地段曾有一所於 1847 年落成的三號警署,於 1903 年拆卸,部分地段建成此郵局,後於 1990 年代初改為環境資源中心環保軒,仍為現存最古老的郵局建築物。圖左方的灣仔峽道當時仍可直通。直到 1949 年,由郵局左面迄至摩理臣山道的一段皇后大道東,亦名為灣仔峽道 (又名「掘斷龍」),同年才併入皇后大道東。(圖片由陳創楚先生提供)

The old Wan Chai Post Office, 1985. The Post Office was opened in 1915.

16
17 | 18

 由灣仔道西望灣仔峽道（皇后大道中），約 1912 年。

右方為於 1858 年落成的第一代灣仔街市（現為屋苑尚翹峰及最新街市）。左方為石水渠街。正中樹叢處曾為三號警署所在，於 1903 年拆卸，部分地段於 1915 年建成灣仔郵局。

Wai Chai Gap Road (merged into Queen's Road East in 1949), c. 1912. The Wan Chai Market is on the right.

落成於 1937 年的第二代灣仔街市，約 2008 年。

這幢包浩斯風格的建築物，即將發展為住宅樓宇壹環。大部分街市外型予以保留，攤檔則遷往最新的街市。

The Wan Chai Market (second generation), c. 2008.

灣仔隆安街玉虛宮（北帝廟），約 1918 年。

這一帶多條街道的地段於 1862 年開投，大部分被華人購入，並集資興建此廟，於 1865 年落成。廟內有原置於九龍城蒲崗村曾富花園內之真武大帝銅像。右方的公所曾被用作於 1949 年創辦的聖雅各兒童會（聖雅各福群會前身）會址。公所右方可見石水渠街的明渠。

Pak Tai Temple on Lung On Street, Wan Chai, c.1918. The stone nullah is on the right.

位於灣仔堅尼地道的聖雅各小學，約 1965 年。

St. James' Primary School, Kennedy Road, Wan Chai, c. 1965.

	21
20	22

 約 1930 年的灣仔。

　　正中為醫院山上的海軍醫院，現為律敦治醫院。其右方為尚未被全部夷平的摩理臣山，其旁是又名「掘斷龍」的灣仔峽道（現為皇后大道東）。右方與堅尼地道交界的山崗上，現時有香港華仁書院，山崗的背後則於 1920 年代初開闢了司徒拔道及連接的黃泥涌峽道和淺水灣道。摩理臣山背後，現伊利沙伯體育館所在，曾於 1940 年代初舉辦工展會。

　　The intersection of Wan Chai Gap Road (Queen's Road East) and Kennedy Road, c. 1930. The Naval Hospital in the middle is where today's Ruttonjee Hospital situated.

 跑馬地馬場，約 1900 年。

香港賽馬活動始於 1844 年，賽馬會則於 1884 年成立。圖正中為主看台，最右方則為草木蓋搭的馬棚。左上方可見稱為「三馬路」的寶雲道。寶雲道與馬場之間的司徒拔道當時尚未闢建。

The Racecourse in Happy Valley, c. 1900.

25 1918 年 2 月 26 日，週年大賽第二天，打吡賽日的下午三時，馬場內草木蓋搭的馬棚發生大火，近 **600 人罹難。大部分遺體被運往加路連山咖啡園的「戊午馬棚中西士女之墓」埋葬。**

A disasterous huge fire engulfed the Racecourse, on Feburary 26, 1918, in which nearly 600 people lost their lives.

24 | 25
     | 26

(26) 日據時期的跑馬地賽馬場，約 1942 年。

三年零八個月日據期間，賽馬活動繼續舉行，跑馬地被改名為「青葉峽」，跑馬場易名為「競馬場」，由何甘棠任理事長。這張經日軍香港憲兵隊檢閱的明信片，約於 1942 年發行，可見當時賽馬的情景，由主看台望向尚未全被夷平之摩理臣山。中間為 1918 年馬棚大火的災場。

The Racecourse during Japanese occupation, c. 1942.

DERBY DAY CATASTROPHE

（濟閱檢隊兵憲港香） 場 馬 競

27 由跑馬地區必列者街（Bridge Street，現為禮頓道）望向堅拿運河（Canal），或稱「鵝澗」，約1915 年。

正中為橫跨運河的寶靈橋（俗稱鵝頸橋）。於 1921 年開展的填海完成後，寶靈橋成為軒尼詩道一部分。左方的堅拿道西可見部分南洋兄弟煙草公司廠房，左方堅拿道東的旁邊有中華糖局（廠）的樓宇和電車廠。該運河於 1960 年代被蓋平以興建往來紅磡海底隧道的交通幹道。

Bowring Canal and Bowrington Bridge (centre), looking from Bridge Street, Happy Valley (today's Leighton Road), c. 1915.

被稱為「鵝頸橋」的一段軒尼詩道旁的「打小人」情景，2006年3月6日驚蟄。

「打小人」勝地由戰前起位於太平山街，1960年代遷往運河旁的禮頓道，約1970年起移至現時地段。早期「打小人」只在驚蟄日舉行，現時則為「年中無休」。求神婆「打小人」的「受眾」，由往時的傳統婦女，延伸至年輕摩登女郎，以及「男人老狗」的漢子，可用「古已有之，於今為烈」來形容。

The traditional ritual of "Jingzhe" on Canal Road, Wan Chai, 2006. A lot of people demand the female devil beaters to "beat away" their enemies, represented by paper effigies, with slippers.

由堅拿道東望向羅素街，約 1969 年。

當時的羅素街兩旁攤檔麋集，右方為電車廠。1980 年代後期，電車廠遷往石塘咀，原址興建時代廣場，於 1990 年代落成。羅素街隨即由雜亂市集，蛻變為全球租值最貴的購物大道。

Russell Street, c. 1969. The tramway depot next to it is where the today's Times Square situated.

30 銅鑼灣軒尼詩道，1954 年。

　　1951 年前，電車由右方波斯富街轉入跑馬地或回廠。有「利舞台」廣告、設有「位元堂夜義學」的一列唐樓，於 1950 年代後期建成軒尼詩大廈，內有中國國貨公司。左方可見一列五層高唐樓，該樓宇是於 1952 年拆卸怡和東倉後興建的，地舖有商務印書館及金馬車飯店。左端亦正興建紐約戲院，於 1955 年落成，所在現為銅鑼灣廣場。

Hennessy Road, 1954. Percival Street is on the right.

LEE GARDEN
HONGKONG

 利園山上榕樹蔭間的中式茶座，約 1928 年。

　　1923 年，商人利希慎購入怡和洋行擁有的渣甸山，易名為利園山，並在此開設一個內有利園戲院的遊樂場。另外，亦在旁邊的波斯富街興建一座利舞台戲院，兩年後落成的遊樂場正中設有中式茶座。1951 年，為配合銅鑼灣填海闢建維多利亞公園，利園山被夷平，泥石用作堆填物。工程完成後，在此開闢了包括蘭芳道、白沙道及啟超道等多條新道路。

Chinese teahouse among banyan trees on the Lee Garden Hill (the former name is Jardine's East Point Hill), c. 1928. The hill was levelled from 1951.

位於軒尼詩道與啟超道之間，被夷平之利園山部分地段上的興利中心，2006年。

　於1979年落成的興利中心，地下及地庫有日資三越百貨。此大廈於2006年開始拆卸，數年後在此落成希慎廣場。

The Mitsukoshi Department Store in Hennessy Centre, on the area of levelled Lee Garden Hill, 2006. The building was later rebuilt into Hysan Place.

33 位於渣甸街與渣甸坊之間，落成於 1952 年的京華戲院，約 1955 年。

京華戲院所在，早期為怡和貨倉及廠房。80 年代改建為京華中心。

Capitol Theatre on Jardine's Bazaar, c. 1955. The theatre was rebuilt into Capitol Centre in 1980s.

34 於 1952 年拆卸渣甸東倉而開闢的一段，由波斯富街至 道延長而成的駱克道，約 1980 年。

街道兩旁為興建於 1952 年的唐樓。正中的華登大廈外可見日資大丸百貨的招牌。

Lockhart Road, looking east from Percival Street, c. 1980. The area was where the original Jardine's Godown situated.

33 | 34

 位於記利佐治街華登大廈內、於 **1960** 年底開業的日資大丸百貨公司，**1962** 年。

這一帶原為渣甸貨倉地段，當時十分僻靜，但附近英皇道及大坑道上，已有大量較高尚的住宅落成，加上百貨公司親切的作風和適度的宣傳，一開業即客似雲來，連同這區亦被「帶旺」。

Daimaru Department Store on Great George Street, c. 1962.

(36) 位於大坑山上的虎豹別墅和萬金油花園，約 1960 年。

　　該別墅和花園於 1936 年 7 月 21 日舉行入伙禮。花園內的泥塑花鳥蟲魚，以及十八層地獄景象，深入民心。和平後的農曆新年期間，每日有數萬人士入內觀看。其白色的虎塔為港島「地標」之一。1988 年，部分花園被改建為住宅樓宇龍華花園。到了 21 世紀初，餘下花園部分亦被改建為高尚住宅屋苑名門，別墅則被保留，保育後重新開放。

The entire view of the Tiger Balm Garden on Tai Hang Road, c. 1960.

 銅鑼灣區鳥瞰圖,約 1996 年。

正中可見掃桿埔運動場及南華會球場。右方可見大坑道旁的豪宅。當時銅鑼灣已十分繁榮。經過 20 年,繁榮程度更加顯著,可用「一日千里」來形容。

The panoramic view of Causeway Bay, c. 1996. The South China Stadium and the So Kon Po Recreation Ground are in the middle.

38 灣仔告士打道，約 1958 年。

　　左中部為與軍器廠街交界的中國艦隊會所（現為中國恒大中心）。左鄰為夏慤大廈，兩旁的前方現為香港演藝學院所在。右中部可見於 1955 年落成的新警察總部堅偉樓，其右方仍見英方軍營及碼頭。

Arsenal Street and Gloucester Road (left), c. 1958. The China Fleet Club and Harcourt House are on the left.

（39）位於灣仔莊士敦道與大王東街之間，一列 19 世紀末期的唐樓，1989 年。

早期這一帶屬於「小東京」，大量日本商店、咖啡室在此開設。和平後轉變為人流不絕的購物區，可見不同類型店舖。約 2005 年，這四座唐樓被重整，保留大押的外貌，其餘部分則被改作吸引遊客的西式食肆。

The Woo Cheong between Johnston Road and Tai Wong Street East, 1989.

40 莊士敦道與汕頭街交界的景象,約1929年。

當時這一帶為外籍娼妓麇集的風月區。煤氣燈旁為一家辦館,其招牌說明是供應外國軍艦的船上伙食者。此風月區因後來洋娼區禁娼令將於1933年實行,一直維持至1932年底。

The intersection of Johnston Road and Swatow Street, c. 1929. This is a foreign prostitute area in Wan Chai.

41 由莊士敦道望向利東街,2006年。

這條早期接近洋娼區的街道,於戰後開有不少洋服店及樓梯舖。由1970年代起,逐漸被不少以婚嫁喜帖為主的印務館取代,故有「喜帖街」之別名。2007年,利東街與及鄰近街道的部分樓宇開始拆卸,並發展為購物、飲食及休憩的步行街。以往喜帖街的特色則已蕩然無存。

Lee Tung Street, also known as "Wedding Card Street", 2006. The street has been transformed into a tree-lined pedestrian walkway, Lee Tung Aveune, nowadays.

 由太原街東望莊士敦道，約 1958 年。

可見位於石水渠街旁，1958 年由龍鳳茶樓轉變的龍門大茶樓，稍後再轉變為設有歌壇的酒樓，惟於 2010 年結業。正中位於灣仔道交界為已拆平的舊二號警署地盤，並即將興建中匯大廈。左方的大成酒家和其背後的一列樓宇，於 1960 年代中被改建為東興大廈及鴻江大廈，曾分別開有中邦國貨公司及新中華國貨公司。近年，三聯書店先後在這兩間公司原址營業。位於正中的馮良記表行的三十年代「石屎」樓宇，現仍存在。

Johnston Road, looking east from Tai Yuen Street, c. 1958. The famous Lung Mun Teahouse is on the middle right.

 由莊士敦道望向茂羅街，2005 年。

　　19 世紀後期，包括茂羅、巴路士及曷（Heard）公司等機構的船廠及機器廠在此開設，是為這一帶街道名稱的由來。左方可見位於 1 號，開業於戰前的有仔記酒家。圖中多幢唐樓與及背後位於巴路士街者，稍後大加整頓，曾變身為「動漫基地」，現改名為「茂羅街七號」。

Mallory Street, looking from Johnston Road, 2005. The Chinese houses in the middle later redeveloped into Comix Homebase, and then renamed as "7 Mallory Street".

1953 年 6 月 2 日，英女皇加冕會景巡遊時，在軒尼詩道與莊士敦道交界油站前萬人空巷的景象。

左方史劍域道口為大澳飯店及灣仔茶樓（現為光華大廈），再隔鄰可見著名的如英印花製罐廠。圖左方多幢興建於 1920 年代填海地段上的三合土四層高唐樓，現時只餘下數幢。（圖片由謝炳奎先生提供）

The parade celebrating the coronation of the Queen Elizabeth II passing through Hennessy Road, June 2, 1953. Stewart Road is on the left.

45 由堅拿道向西望軒尼詩道，約
1951 年。

左方為於 1947 年開業的英男大茶
樓，右方為以魚翅馳名的大三元酒家，
以及曾為鏞記酒家的僑民飯店。由前方
電車起至消防局的一段軒尼詩道，於
1920 年代填海前曾為著名的鵝頸橋。
英男大茶樓前端的堅拿道現為「打小人」
勝地。

Hennessy Road, looking west from
Canal Road, c. 1951. The famous Tai Sam
Yuen Restaurant is on the right.

OISTRICT, HONG KONG.

46 約 1953 年，由軍器廠街至天后區的景象。

正中為修頓球場，可見超過千幢排列整齊、興建於 1930 年的「石屎」樓宇。吉列島（奇力島）已有堤道連接，維多利亞公園填海幾近完成，新避風塘亦在其前方落成。圖左中部可見紅磡灣之黃埔船塢。

Panoramic view of Wan Chai, from the naval dockyard to Tin Hau, c. 1953. The reclamation for the Victoria Park was completed.

47 位於灣仔告士打道 67 號新填地海旁，於 1933 年落成的六國飯店（酒店），1986 年。

　　該酒店在淪陷時期曾易名為東京酒店。1950 年代，酒店右下方有著名的仙掌夜總會，稍後亦有一家甘露夜總會於左下方開設。1986 年 11 月 1 日，六國飯店拆卸重建為新六國酒店。（圖片由何其銳先生提供）

Luk Kwok Hotel (first generation) on no. 67, Gloucester Road, 1986.

48 由灣仔新填地南望告士打道，約 1979 年。

　　左方為菲林明道。可見剛落成的合和中心，左方有 Mido 廣告牌的廣興大廈，稍後連同其右鄰多幢新舊樓宇，被改建為大新金融中心。前方地段曾於 1970 年起舉辦數屆工展會，後於 1980 年代起陸續興建包括華潤大廈、中環廣場、香港會議展覽中心及入境事務大樓等建築物。

Reclamation area and Gloucester Road, Wan Chai, c. 1979. Fleming Road is on the left.

 位於告士打道的灣仔警署，1986 年。

其前身為位於莊士敦道與灣仔道交界，於 1868 年落成的二號警署，後於 1932 年遷至此。右鄰為華國酒店，稍後改建為教會。（圖片由何其銳先生提供）

The Wan Chai Police Station on Gloucester Road, 1986.

灣仔往紅磡海底隧道的交滙處，約 1975 年。

　　當年交通不算繁忙。隧道出入口的左端為吉列島（奇力島）上的遊艇會及警官俱樂部。圖中右方可見位於北角之「角」，即香港電燈公司的舊發電廠和煙囪（所在現為住宅樓宇城市花園）。其右方的屈臣氏大廈現為海景大廈。

The intersection of the Cross Harbour Tunnel, Wan Chai, c. 1975.

 銅鑼灣夜景，約 1968 年。

　　正中為大丸百貨公司所在的華登大廈。其右方為由牛奶公司物業發展而成的珠城大廈。前中部為樂聲戲院及聖斯酒店。左方「勞力士」(Rolex) 廣告牌的背後是豪華戲院大廈。除牛奶公司發展的珠城大廈、恒隆中心及皇室堡外，早期這一帶地段全為怡和洋行所有。

Night view of the East Point area, Causeway Bay, looking from Tai Hang Road, c. 1968.

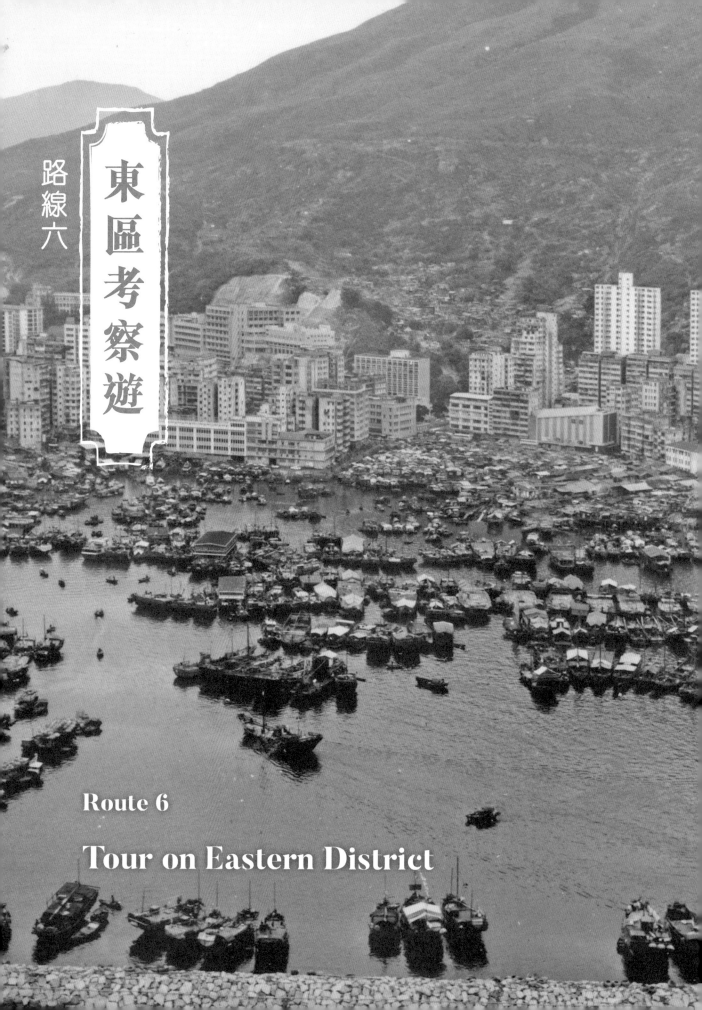

路線六

東區考察遊

Route 6

Tour on Eastern District

前言

東區考察遊一般分作兩段：第一段由天后廟起步，了解天后廟的典故，以及銅鑼灣地名及其別名的源由，又可了解天后山和天后廟道的開闢過程。

之後在銀幕街回顧早期的電影製片廠，還有 1930 年代在這區域夷山開闢英皇道的歷史。

其後，步入早期電車路經的電氣道，探討 1920 年代設於此區的包括化妝品、食品、製榫製罐廠、汽水廠以及油庫等設施。當中最大規模者是 1922 年由灣仔遷至此的發電廠。

由發電廠旁的大強街返回英皇道，可瀏覽皇都戲院和懷緬昔日小上海的繁榮，小上海區的建設始於 1940 年代後。在此區可了解早期的遊樂場「名園」，和戰後的「月園」，還有附近的夜總會、戲院、「海派」食肆、百貨公司、時裝店和理髮店等。

北角區其中一個偉大建築是位於糖水道、英皇道與書局街之間的商務印書館，為 1930 年代該區最宏大的機構。其背後的渣華道則有落成於 1957 年，被稱為「闊佬廉租屋」的北角邨。

此段考察遊的終點在書局街口的新光戲院。

第二段考察遊的起步點，是原來由中華巴士車廠改建的港運城，經過原為電車公司宿舍的健威花園住宅大廈，再步往早期的「七姊妹泳場區」。

迄至 1930 年代中，這一帶的筲箕灣道（英皇道）電車路是單軌者，設有「避車處」以供「對頭車」通過。

健康村迄至鰂魚涌一帶，早期為若干座禾田農舍的村落，對出的海旁則為設有多座泳場棚屋的七姊妹泳場和海灘。其中，最著名的是於 1940 年開業的麗池游泳場，多屆香港小姐選舉均在其舞廳舉辦。「麗池」對面的山腰上有一座二伯公廟，早期有大量塘西等地的風塵女子前往膜拜。

之後，是太古洋行「王國」，包括糖廠、漆廠、船塢及員工宿舍，現時已變為太古坊、太古城、康怡花園及康山花園等商住樓宇羣，部分宿舍則改建為海景樓、益發大廈以及太安樓等住宅。

從西灣河往前走，可試試尋找昔日包括長樂、金星及永華等戲院的原址，踏入稱為「餓人灣」之地，並在興民街與南安街一帶，懷緬昔日筲箕型的海灣，以及早期前往鯉魚門、三家村及茶果嶺之利安小輪碼頭。

　　接着，前往望隆街、工廠街及金華街，了解早期的著名工廠，然後到訪譚公廟和天后廟。考察完畢，可在筲箕灣東大街一帶的食肆品嚐魚蛋粉麵、焗豬扒飯及石斑片炒河等美食。

Introduction

An exploratory trail of Eastern District normally consists of two sections. For the first section, the starting point is at Tin Hau. Participants should seek out tales, tidbits and lores about the area, its nomenclature and examine the origins and development of Tin Hau Temple and the surrounding hilly area, i.e. Ma Shan.

Visitors can check out the history of film making in Ngan Mok Street area and find out as much as possible about the opening up and development of King's Road, which was originally part of Shaukeiwan Road. That part of King's Road was renamed as such in 1935 in honour of the Silver Jubilee of King George V's reign.

Then proceed along Electric Road utilised by the early tramways. The area is rich in heritage and one can explore the nature of the many trades and mini industries established in the 1920's, e.g. cosmetics, aerated drinks bottling plants, eateries and oil depots. The most significant aspect of the area is the setting up by the Hongkong Electric Company of a power generating plant which was transferred from Wanchai in 1922.

Entering centering King's Road via Power Street, one can browse around the State Theatre complex and reminisce about the origins and different facets of "Little Shanghai" which had its origins in the late 1940's. Visitors can search for remnants of the early amusement facilities / establishments, e.g. Ming Yuen and Yuet Yuen, shopping malls, Shanghai-style restaurants, beauty parlous, barber shops and fashion outlets.

A magnificent structure, home to the Commercial Press, the doyen of publication was erected at a spot on King's Road, junction of Tong Shui Road and Shu Kuk Street and had established itself as the largest organisation in the area since the early 1930's. A notable structure along Java Road is the North Point Estate, completed in 1957 and became known as "the subsidised housing for the generous" as residents of several blocks were afforded a magnificent sea view. Another iconic building to explore is the historic Sunbeam Theatre.

The places to explore in the second section include the former depot of the now defunct China Motor Bus Company. The site is now occupied by the residential complex, Island Place (completed in May, 1997). The present-day Healthy Gardens used to be a former tram depot. We then make the way to Tsat Tsz Mui Road, an area which hosted several bathing pavilions, including Hong Kong's largest one.

Up until the mid 1930's, the tram operation between King's Road and Shau Kei Wan was a two-way monorail, double or twin line laybys were set up at various intervals to allow two trams running in opposite directions to pass by on the same line.

In the early pre-development days, the stretch of land extending from Healthy Village to the Quarry Bay area consisted of many rice fields and farming villages. The coastline was home to the previously mentioned swimming pavilions and beaches. The most famous entertainment complex was the Ritz, which comprised a large indoor swimming pool, outdoor swimming facilities, a mini golf course, a skating rink and a fabulous nightclub where quite a few sessions of the annual "Miss Hong Kong Pageant" were held therein. On the hill opposite the aforementioned facilities stood the Yee Pak Kung Temple where many ladies of the night paid their respects and sought solutions to their earthly problems.

Next, one can take a journey into the past and visualise the business sites run by the Swire Group, i.e. sugar refineries, paint works, dockyard facilities and the provision of staff quarters. All these places have now been replaced by the Taikoo Place, Taikoo Shing, Kornhill and the Kornhill Plaza which are for residential cum commercial purposes. Part of the staff quarters have now been morphed into the Harbour View Gardens, Yick Fat Building and Tai On Building.

Flowing eastwards towards Sai Wan Ho, one may try to locate the former sites of long gone theatres such as Cheung Lok (1924-1969), Golden Star and Wing Wah Theatre. Visitors can then enter the Shau Kei Wan / Aldrich Bay area which in very early times was known as "Ngor Yan Wan" (Bay of starving men). Legend has it the name came about, after a group of British merchants were marooned in the area following a typhoon in the 18th century, only to find that there was no food to buy in the area. Times have changed and there are eateries galore in the whole area. At Nam On Street and Hing Man Street one can endeavour to throw our minds back to the pre-reclamation days when the shape of the coastline resembled a sieve or colander made of bamboo strips. Finally, check out the arrangements to reach Lei Yue Mun, Sam Ka Tsuen and Cha Kwo Lung by ferry and landing at the Lei On motor ferry boat pier.

Then linger around Mong Lung Street, Factory Street and Kam Wa Street and imagine in the old days the many factories that were set up here, e.g. Fung Keung Shoe Factory. Lastly, seek divine blessing by visiting the nearby Tam Kung Temple and Tin Hau Temple. At the end of the tour participants can patronise the various eateries especially along Shau Kei Wai Main Street East. The choice of cuisine and menu is endless but many may opt for such traditional favourites like fishballs with noodles or wide flat rice noodles, cooked pork chop rice or stirred fried garoupa slices with rice noodles. Bon Appetit!

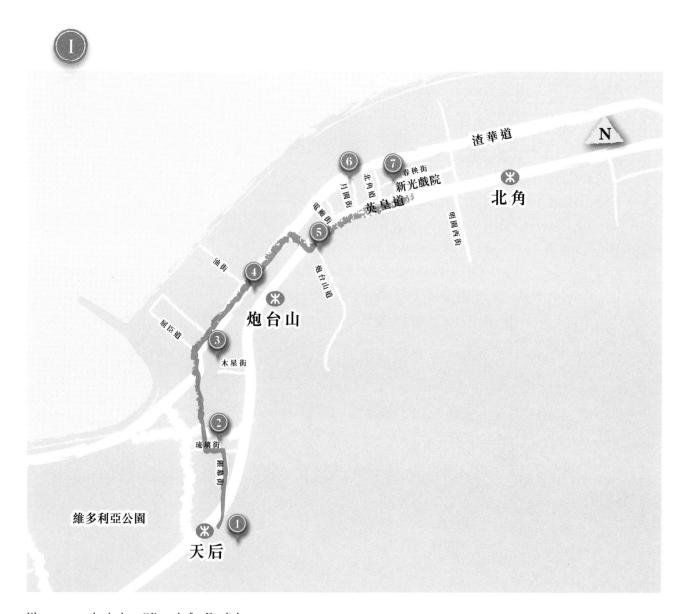

Please scan the below QR code for English map.

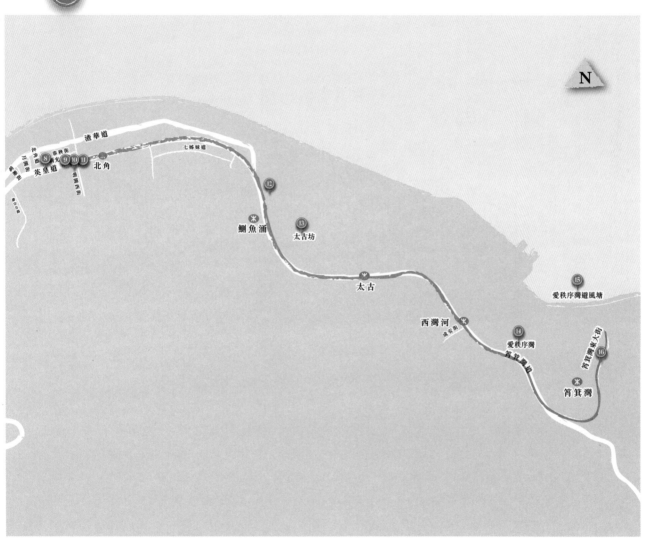

Please scan the below QR code for English map.

Hongkong
"Kun Yum" Temple, Causeway Bay

 銅鑼灣天后廟,約 1900 年。

　　此座於 1841 年開埠前落成的古廟,早期已有紅色及銅製的香爐,因此當時的銅鑼灣亦有「紅香爐」或「銅香爐」的別名。其東邊的地段亦因此廟而定名為天后區。1920 年代初,有一民新製片公司在「天后廟側」攝製電影,故這處有一條銀幕街。片場旁有一個山崗,頂端有一座岳王廟。1935 年,岳王廟他遷,山崗被夷平以開闢英皇道。1936 年,電車亦由行駛筲箕灣道 (電氣道) 改為行經英皇道。

Tin Hau Temple, Causeway Bay, c. 1900.

 1963 年，由天后區望向銅鑼灣。

　　左中部可見百德新街一帶由怡和及卜內門貨倉改建的住宅羣，該地段與維多利亞公園之間，仍有一條供牛奶冰廠輸送冰塊的運河，該運河於數年後蓋平，現為柏寧酒店等樓宇前的一段告士打道。前方左邊的裁判署現為屋苑柏景臺。中部與琉璃街交界的建築是位於 40 號、由馬寶山餅乾廠改建的維景大廈。

The Victoria Park and Causeway Bay district, looking from Tin Hau Temple Road, c. 1963.

 1906 年 9 月 18 日,一場致命颸風後的天后區筲箕灣道(電氣道)。

電車所在約為現時的木星街及屈臣道一帶。

A tram on Shau Kei Wan Road (today's Electric Road near Watson Road), after a disastrous typhoon on September 18, 1906.

4 從油街東望英皇道，約 1960 年。

　　正中為皇都戲院，其背後已建成璇宮大廈。左中部可見被夷平石山的地段，正在興建南方大廈及南天大廈。

The State Theatre on King's Road, looking from Oil Street, c. 1960.

 由炮台山道東望英皇道，1954 年。

左方與電廠街交界，於 1952 年開業的璇宮戲院，於 1958 年易名皇都戲院。其東鄰的熙和街口有一天宮夜總會，其旁四層高樓宇的牆壁上，有「大世界遊樂場」（前身為月園遊樂場）的字樣。右方六層高者，是內有夜總會及酒樓的雲華大廈。其旁邊長康街前的石山，於 1959 年被爆破夷平，約三年後建成五洲大廈。左方的石山亦同時轉變為南方大廈及南天大廈。

The Empire Theatre (renamed as State Theatre in 1958), looking from Fortress Hill Road, c. 1954.

 月圓遊樂場位於渣華道的另一個入口。左方為月圓街,約 1950 年。

The entrance of Luna Amusement Park on Java Road, North Point, c. 1950.

 在戰後填海地段上開闢之春秧街，1981 年。

　　50 年代初，街道左邊與及背接英皇道的地段上，共建有 40 幢樓宇，因此這一帶常被稱為「四十間」。街道兩旁麇集肉類蔬果店舖和攤檔，直到現時仍為一個「人車爭路」的繁囂市集。（圖片由何其銳先生提供）

Chun Yeung Street, a market street in North Point, 1981.

由北角道東望英皇道，1953 年。

這一帶為「小上海」中心點，名店及食肆林立。左方為部分稱為「四十間」的新建樓宇，其東鄰中左方較矮的樓房是龐大的商務印書館，其對面是興建中的都城戲院，所在現為新都城大廈。當時，不少南來的內地人士居於此處，因此迄至 1960 年代初，這一帶較銅鑼灣為繁盛。

King's Road, looking east from North Point Road, 1953. The printing factory of the Commercial Press is at the junction of Shu Kuk Street (middle left).

 位於筲箕灣道（英皇道）、明園西街以東的名園遊樂場，攝於 1918 年剛開業時。

名園遊樂場內有酒店、飲食場所及表演場地，不少人在此舉辦西式或集體婚禮。該遊樂場亦開辦一條前往「塘西風月區」的巴士路線。可是自 1923 年起，名園頻頻倒閉和易手經營，到了 1936 年正式結束營業。其背後的山段亦被稱為名園山。

The Ming Yuen Amusement Park in North Point, c. 1918.

 名園遊樂場的端陽競渡，約 1923 年。

左方的兩座建築物均有「名園」的字樣。右方的名園山頂端有一賽西湖水塘。該山段後來闢建明園西街。龍舟所在的海段現為糖水道一帶。

A dragon boat competition in front of Ming Yuen Amusement Park, c. 1923.

 1966 年 6 月 12 日嚴重雨災期間的明園西街。

從名園山上賽西湖水塘滿溢的洪水，將停泊於明園西街的汽車沖至七歪八倒，疊成一堆。

Cars piled up on Ming Yuen Western Street, after a rainstorm on June 12, 1966.

 約落成於 1960 年的新麗池花園大廈，大廈部分為酒店，內設泳池，為當時高消費遣興場所。

麗池花園大廈前身是位於鰂魚涌的麗池游泳場，在 1940 年開業，場內有泳池及露天泳棚，和平後加設舞廳和夜總會，並曾舉辦多屆「香港小姐」選舉。

New Ritz Hotel with a swimming pool on King's Road, Quarry Bay, c. 1960.

 鰂魚涌，約 1935 年。

　　右方的筲箕灣道約兩年後改名為英皇道。可見於 1882 年興建的太古糖廠及漆廠壘，所在現為太古坊等商業樓宇。左中部為位於鰂魚涌角於 1907 年落成的太古船塢。1973 年，太古船塢與黃埔船塢合併，並遷往青衣，船塢原址闢建為商住樓宇羣太古城。

The Taikoo sugar refinery, paint factory and dockyard in Quarry Bay, c. 1935.

 約 1925 年的愛秩序灣。

因海灣形似「筲箕」(竹織盛物盆籃)
而名為筲箕灣。早期因往來中環交通不
便，必需品只能自給自足，所以又有「餓
人灣」的別名。右下方為阿公岩。正中為
太古船塢和寫字樓，其左鄰為太祥街至
太安街一帶的職員宿舍。

Taikoo dockyard, Sai Wan Ho and
Aldrich Bay (centre), looking from Sau Kei
Wan Main Street East, c. 1925.

 筲箕灣區愛秩序灣避風塘，約 1975 年。

正中為巴士總站，其右鄰為位於南安里交界的永華戲院。左方可見廉租屋邨明華大廈。

Typhoon shelter in Aldrich Bay, Shau Kei Wan, c. 1975.

由電車總站向東望筲箕灣東大街，1985 年。

　　當時仍為一漁村小鎮式街道，有多間傳統糧油店和金舖，當中以天天及泰盛金舖較為知名，現時仍有一間位於左方超級市場隔鄰的漢和。由 1990 年起，筲箕灣東大街逐漸變為美食店舖雲集的「食街」，人流不絕。（圖片由陳創楚先生提供）

Shops and stalls on Shau Kei Wan Main Street East, 1985.

路線七

電車遊

Route 7

Tram Tour

前言

電車於 1904 年開始通車，路線由堅尼地城至筲箕灣，並有一條支線進入跑馬地。進入跑馬地的道路早期是天樂里，1930 年代為堅拿道，到了 1951 年再改為波斯富街。

東區的電車路線早期經電氣道，由該處至筲箕灣原本是單軌路，需設「避車處」。到了 1936 年由電氣道改為英皇道，大部分路段亦改為雙軌。

筲箕灣終點站早期位於筲箕灣道與工廠街交界，1930 年代延長至筲箕灣東大街口。

而堅尼地城的總站，早期位於菜市場前的加多近街，隨即轉入滿佈工廠、貨倉及船廠的吉席街和堅彌地城海旁。

石塘咀總站前的山道、德輔道西和皇后大道西，直到 1930 年代中為「城開不夜」的塘西風月區。附近位於屈地街山邊的煤氣鼓，以及近海的永安貨倉，曾先後發生爆炸和火災，釀成重大傷亡。

經過由海員之家及聖彼得教堂改建落成的新七號差館，便進入早期為鹹魚欄的海味街，

跟着是南北行街（文咸西街）與永樂街一帶的「三角碼頭」區。過了上環街市及已消失的「平民夜總會」（現為信德中心），電車經過找換店雲集之急庇利街，轉入德輔道中。迄至 1970 年代初，這一帶為私娼麕集的廉價「人肉市場」。

迄至 1960 年代在熱鬧的德輔道中（電車路），觸目所見是著名的銀龍、新光、新紀元、大同、金龍及中國等酒家，以及龍記、公團、陸海通及奕樂園等食肆；還有永安、大新、瑞興、先施、協昌及利源等大小百貨公司。多家表行，加上新世界影戲院，使這一帶成為華人的高級消費及宴飲區。

畢打街以東是銀行區，發鈔銀行有利、渣打、滙豐及中國銀行皆位於此。此地段亦為置地公司的商業樓宇「王國」。

過了花園道，便進入下環的皇后大道東（現為金鐘道），兩旁是軍營和船塢，豎有多面紅底白字寫上「不准擅進，如敢故違，開槍射擊」的警告牌，有「生人勿近」的恐怖感。一直到「大佛口」看到「麗的呼聲」廣播電台，氣氛才告緩和。

由晏頓街的「紅磚屋」(海員及海軍會所)一直到克街油站的一段莊士敦道,有包括拍賣行、金舖、書局、押店、茶莊及燒臘店,還有包括龍鳳(龍門)、雙喜、英京、大成等茶樓和酒家。加上這一帶的麗都、金城、東城、東方、環球及國泰等電影院,形成一個人流不絕的繁囂市集。

軒尼詩道上亦有多家包括新亞怪魚、頤園、龍圖(百樂門)及大三元等著名酒家食肆。過了波斯富街則有包括金馬車餐廳、寶芳鞋王及商務印書館等名店。由 1960 年代起,此地段逐漸轉變為最繁盛的飲食和購物區,當中亦有多家包括利舞台(1925-1991)、紐約、京華(1952-1977)、樂聲(1949-1974)及豪華(1954-1981)等氣派一流的影院。

之後,便進入避風塘(維多利亞公園)旁的高士威道,現中央圖書館及皇仁書院一帶的地段,早期為馬球場及皇后遊樂場。此地段於開埠初期還未填海時,連同避風塘,為一銅鑼型海灣,是故有「銅鑼灣」一名。高士威道(Causeway)原是設於銅鑼型海灣正中,以方便行人往來的堤道。

電車早期經過之電氣道,名稱源自 1922 年由灣仔日街、月街、星街一帶遷至的香港電燈公司發電廠(現為城市花園屋苑所在)。過了發電廠,則為繁盛的「小上海」(現為「小福建」)

區域,商務印書館的廠址現為華豐國貨及新光戲院所在的僑冠大廈及僑輝大廈。

中華巴士的車廠於 1990 年代改建為港運城,再過去是由農耕地段轉變而成的平民屋健康村及模範邨。對開為七姊妹泳場海段,其名稱源於早期一塊突出於水面、形如七人相擁一起的大石。因形狀亦似七人聚在一起猜枚,故早期該區亦有「七子枚」之名。

1880 年,當局將一大片被形容為「人跡罕至」的地段,批予太古洋行興建糖廠。該地段被名為打石灣及鰂魚涌;稍後再批出一片位於鰂魚涌角及黃角咀的地段,供太古洋行興建船塢。兩者於 1970 年代起陸續重整和發展,由人跡罕至的區域,演變為日夜人流不絕的住宅及商業消費區。

與其相連的西灣河和早期稱為「餓人灣」的筲箕灣,直到 1970 年代仍不脫邊陲市集及漁港之特色。隨後,柴灣區大力發展,東區走廊開通,作為柴灣、石澳、大潭以至赤柱等地中轉站的筲箕灣,亦日趨繁盛,與鰂魚涌、太古城等一帶的熱鬧程度相比,不遑多讓。

Introduction

In 1904, the trams provided services from Kennedy Town to Shau Kei Wan, with an extension to Happy Valley (Yue Yuen). Access to Happy Valley initially was by way of Tin Lok Lane. In 1930, Canal Road was used for the purpose and then finally the extension ran through Percival Street.

During the early services to the Eastern area, trams ran on Electric Road using a single-track system all the way to Shau Kei Wan, and hence double line laybys had to be set up at various intervals. In 1936, that part of Shau Kei Wan Road was renamed King's Road and a double-track system was adopted.

The early tram services ended at a terminus situated between Shau Kei Wan Road and Factory Street. In 1930, the line was extended to the initial section of Shau Kei Wan Main Street East.

The early Kennedy Town line terminated at a stop near the Cadogan Street Vegetable Wholesale Market. The trams travelled along Catchick Street and Praya Kennedy Town where factories, godowns and small-scale ship repair shops proliferated.

The tram service also covered the area around Hill Road, Des Voeux Road West and Queen's Road West, and in the 1930's, this sector was a flourishing brothel area known as "Shek Tong Tsui" red light district and aptly dubbed "the City that never sleeps". On May 14, 1934, a huge explosion of a gasometer at the West Point coal gas plant (Whitty Street) caused quite a few fatalities and a subsequent fire at the Wing On Godown resulted in many casualties.

The line proceeded along the tracks past the former "Sailors' Home" and the newly constructed no. 7 Police Station which stood on the site of the former Saint Peter's Church. Visitors can then enter that part of Des Voeux Road West, popularly known as "salted fish market" which has transformed itself into the modern / present-day "dried seafood street". Participants can go to the so-called Nam Pak Hong Street, literally meaning South-north Trading Hongs (companies). The area is represented by Bonham Strand West. An important landmark of the area is the so-called Triangular Pier which is at the end of Wing Lok Street. The proper name for the pier is the Wing Lok Street Wharf. We then make our way past the former Western Market and the long defunct "Poor Man's Nightclub" (at present-day Shun Tak

Centre). The working class populace visited to buy cheap goods, eat inexpensive but delicious street foods and enjoyed the various forms of entertainment available. The trams then trudge into Cleverly Street, home to numerous money-changing shops. The area was quite saturated with many female street-walkers right up to the 1970's.

We are then on Des Voeux Road Central where many famous restaurants and teahouses carried on their flourishing trade. Names such as Ngun Lung, Sun Kwong, Sun Kie Yuen, Tai Tung, Kam Lung and Chung Kwok evoke pleasant memories. Other famous eateries are Lung Kee, Kung Tuen, Luk Hoi Tung and Yik Lok Yuen. Moreover, modern and high-class department stores abounded, namely Wing On, the Sun Company, Shui Hing, Sincere, Heep Cheong and Lay Yuen. With the proliferation of watch and jewellery shops, plus the magnificent "World Theatre", the area soon grew into a glittering shopping, dining and entertainment mecca for the local population.

East of Peddar Street was the financial and banking sector where note-issuing banks, i.e. the Mercantile Bank, the Chartered Bank, the presently named HSBC and the Bank of China congregated

in that sector. The area was the core of Hong Kong Land's commercial and property empire.

Going past Garden Road, we enter Queen's Road East (present-day Queensway) in "Ha Wan". On both sides of this section were established military barracks and a naval dockyard with prominent warning signs erected. The white lettering against a red background read: "WARNING – MILITARY AREA – NO ENTRY". The tension in the air only eases when one approaches Dai Fut Hau and the former Rediffusion Studio.

After Hennessy Road was built, the red-bricked "Sailors' & Soldiers' Home" was situated at the corner of Hennessy Road and Anton Street (1929). Along this stretch of Johnston Road right up to the petroleum station near Heard Street were established auction houses, jewellery shops, bookshops, pawn shops, tea wholesalers and Chinese barbecued meat shops. Restaurants and teahouses abounded, e.g. Lung Fung (Lung Moon), Sheung Hei (Double Happiness), Ying King (very exclusive) and Tai Shing, plus the conglomeration of theatres, e.g. Lido (Landale Street), Golden City, East Town, the Oriental, the Globe (1950-1971) and Cathay Theatre (1939-

1984). All these establishments constituted to create a thriving, flourishing and bustling bazaar atmosphere.

Likewise, restaurants and teahouses blossomed, e.g. Sun Ya Kwai Yu Restaurant, Yee Yuen, Lung Tol (Pak Lok Moon) and Tai Sam Yuen. Walking past Percival Street, we come into contact with the former locations of famous establishments namely, the Golden Carriage Restaurant, Po Fong Shoes Shop and the branch of the Commercial Press. From the early 1960's, this stretch of Wanchai / Causeway Bay had gradually but magically become one of the most popular and thriving dining, shopping and entertainment hubs of the city. Practically, all of the most pleasant memories of the magnificent and elegant theatres existing then are forever embedded in our minds and heart. They include the Lee Theatre (1925-1991), New York, Capitol (1952-1977), Roxy Theatre (1949-1974) and Hoover Theatre (1954-1981), and all of them were in a distinct class of their own genre.

After being mesmerized by this magical hotspot, visitors can then move on to the Causeway Bay Typhoon Shelter (the present-day Victoria Park) along Causeway Road and then the Central Public Library comes into sight. The site of the library and the stretch of open field right up to the present campus of Queen's College used to be a military / government sports ground cum polo field. The Chinese name for Causeway Bay is "Tung Lo Wan", meaning Copper Gong Bay which is the bay at the seaward end of the So Kon Po valley. The Chinese name refers to the shape of the bay which resembled a broken copper gong. The English named the bay after the breakwater / causeway built across the shallow inlet.

In the early days, trams ran along Electric Road which got its name from the setting up by the Hongkong Electric Company of a power generating plant (the present-day City Gardens), which was transferred from the cluster around Sun Street, Moon Street and Star Street in Wanchai. On entering King's road we come into an area known as "Little Shanghai" which is now somewhat overshadowed by another group of immigrants, the Fujianese and hence the area is now better known as "Little Fujian", the centre of activity revolves around Chun Yeung Street. A magnificent structure is the premises of the sprawling Commercial Press. The premises are now largely occupied by the Wah Fung Chinese Goods Centre located in Kiu Kwan Mansion and next to Kiu Fai Mansion.

The former depot of the now defunct China Motor Bus Company is now occupied by the residential complex, Island Place (completed in May 1997). Further east where paddy fields abounded are two public housing estates: Healthy Village and Model Housing Estate. Towards the coastline were the coastal Tsat Tsz Mui swimming pavilions. The name originates from the shape of seven boulders embracing each other. Another folklore has it that a big boulder had the appearance of seven persons engaged in "a Chinese finger-guessing drinking game". The boulder was only visible during low tides before the entire area was reclaimed.

In 1880, the Government granted a big piece of desolate land to the then Butterfield and Swire Company (the Swire Group nowadays) to build a sugar refinery. The present Quarry Bay area was a bay where rock from the hillsides were quarried. The Cantonese name "Tsak Yue Chung" reveals that it was a small stream where crucian carp could be found in the 19th century. The eastern part of Quarry Bay, namely "Quarry Point" was largely owned by Swire and Taikoo Dockyard began operations in 1907. In the early 1970's, the Swire Group decided to restructure their holdings in the area. Subsequently, the land (mainly dockyard area) was used to develop a large private housing estate, Taikoo Shing, a bristling residential complex with commercial and retail outlets.

However, the Sai Wan Ho, Shau Kei Wan and Aldrich Bay area retained, until the mid 1970's, their characteristics as a rural market and fishing village outpost. With the subsequent massive development of Chai Wan and the completion the Eastern Corridor, Shau Kei Wan and the neighbouring area became a focal point of interchange covering the Shek O, Tai Tam and Stanley sub-districts. It soon developed into a flourishing and bustling mini-metropolis and in every way reminiscent of the more modern part of Taikoo Shing and Quarry Bay which are sometimes referred to as "Central East".

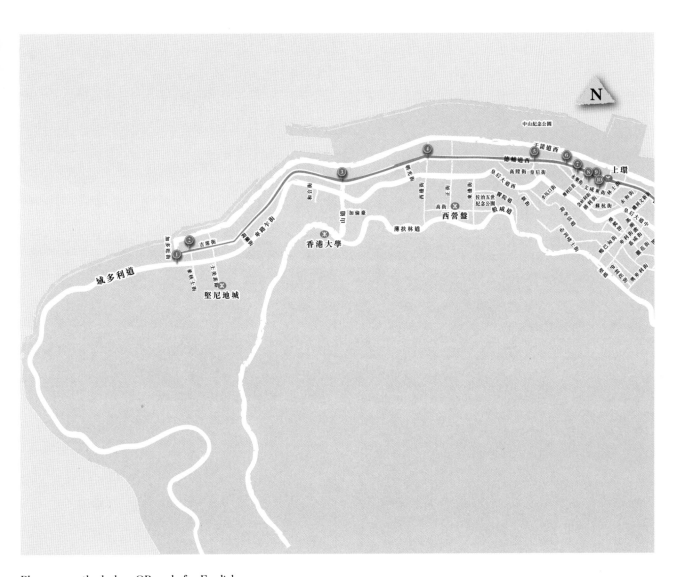

Please scan the below QR code for English map.

（續）(contunued)

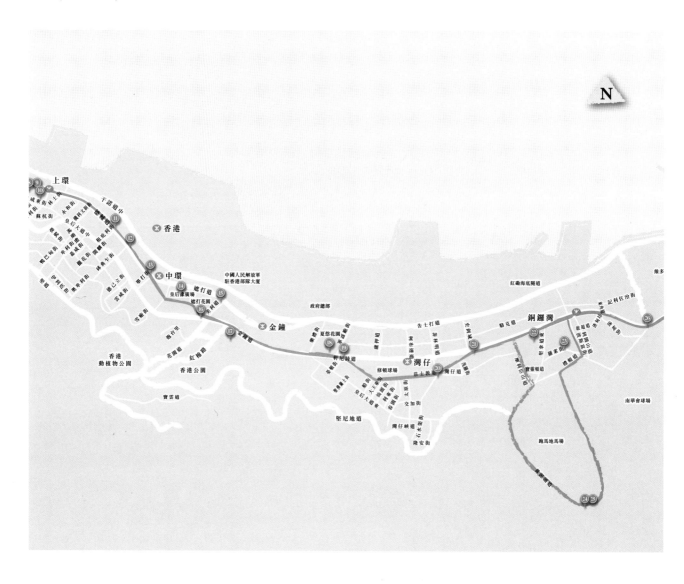

（續）(contunued)

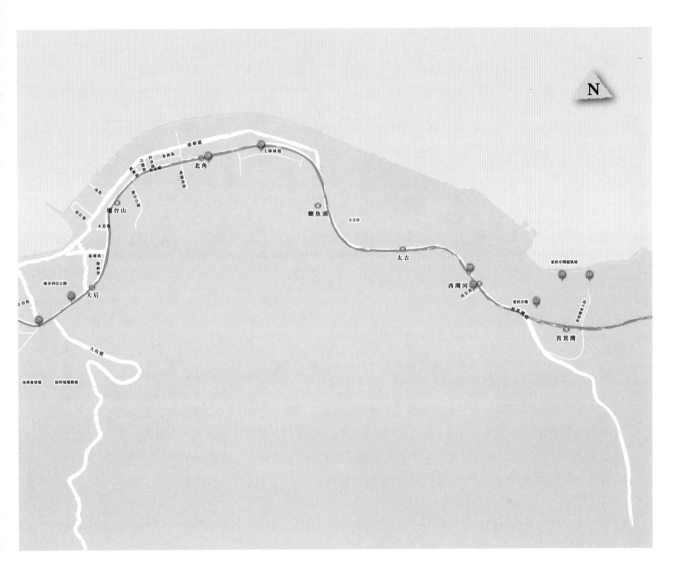

e Pergola in Kennedy Town of H.K.

 約 1930 年，位於西環堅尼地城域多利道與加多近街交界的一別亭。

於 1903 年落成的域多利道，是為紀念維多利亞女皇（Queen Victoria）登基六十週年而開闢的。一別亭由東華醫院於 1918 年興建，是供早期出殯巡行中送殯的友好向逝者作最後致祭與道別，有「送君千里，終須一別」之意。1950 年前後，東華醫院曾在一別亭的範圍，安置由內地來港的難民。其所在現時為東華三院的百年大樓。

A pavilion built by Tung Wah Hospital for funeral attendees in 1918, at the intersection of Victoria Road and Cadogan Street, c. 1930.

 西環吉席街（當時名為遮打街）與爹核士街（右）交界，約 1903 年。

當時該處正舖設電車軌。電車後於 1904 年通車。

The intersection of Chater Street (later renamed as Catchick Street in 1909) and Davis Street (right), c. 1903. The tram tracks were being laid.

248

3 德輔道西與山道交界的石塘咀電車總站，約 1908 年。

可見兩部最早的電車。圖中的廣東大酒店於 1911 年變為陶園酒家。這家位於「塘西風月區」的一級宴飲聚樂場所，一直經營至淪陷時期。和平後的 1950 年代中，被改作可與長江公司塑膠廠分庭抗禮的香港人造花廠。約 1980 年再被改建為香港商業中心。

Kwong Tung Hotel (later changed to Tao Yuen Restaurant in 1911) at the intersection of Hill Road and Des Voeux Road West, and the tramway terminal at Shek Tong Tsui, c. 1908.

④ 於1864年落成,位於海旁西(德輔道西)接近西邊街的「些那堪」(Sailors' Home,海員之家,又稱「水手館」),約1918年。

該館曾於1910年在灣仔大佛洋行左旁開設新館。「些那堪」於1950年代初與東鄰的聖彼得教堂同被拆卸,於1955年建成新七號差館(西區警署)。

The Sailors' Home, built on Des Voeux Road West in 1864, c. 1915. The building was demolished together with Saint Peter's Church on its left, to make room for the new Western District Police Station.

⑤ 由皇后街西望德輔道西「鹹魚欄」的中心點，約 1930 年。

　　兩旁有多家鹹魚店、蒲包（蔴包）店及藥店。最左面的一幢是南洋煙草公司第三義學，其右鄰是雲香大茶樓。該茶樓稍後遷往皇后大道中 46 號武彝仙館原址。上述義學及茶樓所在，約為現時的蓮香居茶樓。

Centre point of "salty fish market street" on Des Voeux Road West, looking west from Queen Street, c. 1930.

6 停泊省港澳內河船的永樂街碼頭，
約 1925 年。

　　碼頭數年後改名為永樂碼頭。因其
位於德輔道西（前）與干諾道西（右中）
的 L 型「轉角位」，所以被稱為「三角碼
頭」。圖中可見拉拽滿載白米的木頭車，
以及手持「擔挑」（竹竿）被稱為「三角碼
頭咕喱」的搬運工人。這一帶迄至修打蘭
街的地段，亦被稱為「三角碼頭區」。該
碼頭於 1960 年代後期被拆卸，所在約為
現時的西消防街。

Coolies and porters on Connaught
Road West, c. 1925. The Wing Lok Street
Wharf, also known as "Triangular Pier," is
on the left.

 由北便上環街市西望干諾道西，約 1925 年。

電車背後是「三角碼頭」。右方有一座由英商營辦、供內河船廣東號、廣西號及泉州號等停泊的碼頭。

Hotels and piers on Connaught Road West, looking west from Western Market on Morrison Street, c. 1925.

位於干諾道西的北便上環街市，1985 年。

　　落成於 1906 年的北便上環街市，在淪陷時期易名為「昭和市場」，用作批售瓜菜予攤販。1991 年，街市大加整頓，改變為設有酒樓、食肆及購物商場的西港城。二樓是來自原來「花布街」（永安街）的店舖，清一色售賣布疋呢絨。（圖片由陳創楚先生提供）

The Western Market on Connaught Road West, 1985. The market was converted into a shopping arcade with restaurants in 1991.

 由上環街市（西港城）東望德輔道中及上環電車總站，約 1950 年。

　　左方可見陸海通飯店、新國民及璇宮餐室，另有一間馬寶山餅乾廠門市部。迄至 1970 年代初，這一帶仍是私娼麇集的「人肉市場」。

Low grade hotels and brothels on Des Voeux Road Central, Sheung Wan, looking from the Western Market, c. 1950.

CENTRAL DISTRICT H.K.

 約 1950 年，由 東望德輔道中。

左方可見於 1920 年代開業的嘉華銀行（現為中信銀行）。遞邅益單車行隔鄰是以「葉牌恤」馳名的
同益製衣廠。正中禧利街兩旁有以燒鵝馳名的公團飯店，以及俄國菜館龍記。右方有金時鞋廠的建築
是雙妹嘜廣生行化妝品老店。正中可見大同酒家的招牌，酒家所在現時為中信銀行。圖片正中依次是
永安公司、新世界戲院、瑞興公司及大新公司。

Des Voeux Road Central, looking east from Cleverly Street, c. 1950. Wing On Company, The Sun
Company and Sincere Company are at the centre.

Des Veoux

258

& Electric Car.
gkong

 由臨時影畫場（現為恒生銀行）西望德輔道中，約 1905 年。

左方為租庇利街及中環街市。租庇利街與及其右鄰的部分樓宇於 1883 年之前為鐵行輪船公司大樓。這一列唐樓大部分於 1920 年代改為大觀酒店，在酒店背後有一條鐵行里。

A tram on Des Voeux Road Central, near Central Market and Jubilee Street (left), c. 1905.

254 DES-VOEUX ROAD H.K.

 由砵典乍街東望德輔道中,約 1933 年。

　　左方的一間信行金銀公司,以西式技術化煉黃金白銀而馳名。再隔鄰是工商日、晚報社及其附屬的《天光報》社址,所在現為招商永隆銀行。圖中最高的鐵行大廈現為歐陸中心。正中有圓形屋頂的廣東銀行大廈,現為中國建設銀行(亞洲)。

Des Voeux Road Central, looking east from Pottinger Street, c. 1933. The tallest building at the centre is the P&O Building.

1870 年代的畢打街。

正中為落成於 1862 年、位於皇后大道中交界的鐘塔。該鐘塔兼具報火警功能，於 1912 年因阻塞交通而被拆除。左方的整列屋宇，是由顛地洋行變身的香港大酒店，於 1867 年開業。樹叢右方是郵政總局，於 1924 年改建為華人行。右方渣甸行（怡和大樓）的座柱上，有「海旁中街」（Praya Central）的路牌。海旁中街約於 1895 年易名為德輔道中。

Pedder Street and the clock tower, looking from Praya Central (later renamed as Des Voeux Road Central, c. 1895), 1870s. Hong Kong Hotel is on the left while Jardine House is on the right.

14 **由干諾道中望向皇后像廣場，1961 年 11 月。**

可見部分廣場仍被用作停車場。正中部分蓋有一座懸掛紅燈籠的竹牌樓，連同滙豐銀行及渣打銀行的裝飾，均是用作歡迎訪港的英國雅麗珊郡主。

Statue Square and bank area, looking from Connaught Road Central, November, 1961. The decoration was to welcome the visit of Princess Alexandra to Hong Kong.

15 **由美利道望皇后大道中，約 1925 年。**

左方為花園道口之美利操場及其前端的公廁。右方的木球會現為遮打花園，其背後的大會堂於1951 年改建為中國銀行大廈。

The City Hall on Queen's Road Central, looking west from Murray Road, c. 1925.

16 **殯喪巡行正經過皇后大道中的木球會（左）及美利操場（右），約 1930 年。**

在花園道的交通亭頂可見 "GO" 的指示牌。電車所在是皇后大道東的起點，約於 1970 年易名為金鐘道。中上方可見海軍船塢的煙囪。

Funeral parade passing through Queen's Road Central, c. 1930. The Murray Parade Ground is on the right.

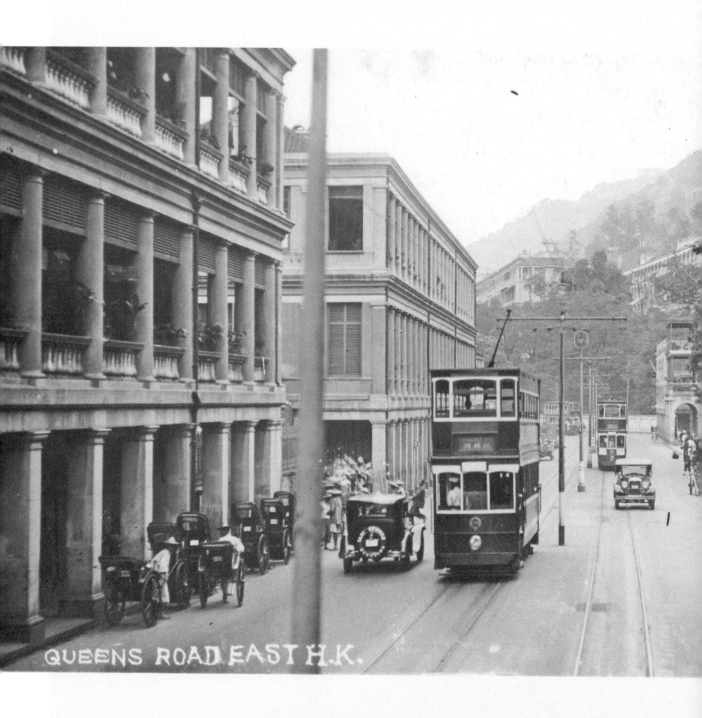

QUEENS ROAD EAST H.K.

 約 1930 年的皇后大道東（金鐘道）。

　　電車左方為海軍船塢入口，直至 1950 年代，每當下午五、六時下班時段，五、六千名工人魚貫而出，道路兩旁變得十分擠擁。圖右方於 1890 年代時仍有街道包括「洋貨街」（又名「廣州市場」，Canton Bazaar）、「金些厘巷」（Commissariat Lane）及「啟明里」（Kai Ming Lane），還有一條約 1970 年消失的蟠龍里（Broom Lane）。右方為美利軍營，正中為域多利軍營，所在現為太古廣場及酒店羣。右中部現為高等法院所在。

Queen's Road East (Queensway), c. 1930. The entrance of the naval dockyard is on the left. The greenery on the right is the site of the nowaday's High Court.

威靈頓軍營內的樂禮大樓，約 1915 年。

其三角屋簷上的金色字樣和指針時鐘，為市民「認可」的地標，故稱這一帶為「金鐘」，一如附近的「大佛口」。約 1970 年，這一帶的皇后大道東亦改名為金鐘道。同時，樂禮大樓亦重建，於 1980 年代再度拆卸，以開闢夏愨花園。其旁也開闢了一條樂禮街。

Rodney House inside the Wellington Barrack, c. 1915. The Chinese name of Admiralty, "Kam Chung" came from the golden clock of Rodney House.

 約 1918 年的灣仔海旁東。

左上方海軍設施的左旁，是第一代軍器廠街，圖中亦可見泊於遠處的白色添馬軍艦。中前方是大佛碼頭，電車的左方是晏頓街。1921 年開展的填海，於 1930 年完成後，而這一段海旁東後來易名為莊士敦道。

Praya East, Wan Chai, looking west from Fenwick Street, c. 1918. The first generation Arsenal Street is at the back of the tram.

 1950 年的莊士敦道。

左方是灣仔道，可見大鴻運酒店及著名的和玉燒臘店。電車頂部亦見祺棧茶莊及「西法接生所」的招牌。而右方「鍾二姑接生」的招牌背後，為與菲林明道交界的英京大酒家，所在現為大有廣場。

The intersection of Johnston Road, Wan Chai Road (left) and Fleming Road (right), c. 1950. The Ying King Restaurant to the right is where the today's Tai Yau Building situated.

18 | 19
20

266

310 WELLINGTON BARRACK

21 莊士敦道（右中部）與軒尼詩道交界，
1953 年。

　　第一部電車後方之克街兩旁，有兩
間學校及一間中醫學院。左方可見於戰
後開業、以太爺雞馳名的頤園大酒家。
史劍域道口兩旁，有大澳飯店和灣仔茶
樓。右下方為加德士油站的樓宇。（曾
在此任職的集郵界前輩謝炳奎先生，於
1953 年英女皇加冕出會巡遊經過這一帶
時，攝得多幀精彩照片，我獲他惠贈若
干張，感激莫名。）

The intersection of Hennessy Road,
Johnston Road (right) and Stewart Road
(left), c. 1953.

65. HENNESSY ROAD, HONG KONG.

22 由寶靈頓道東望軒尼詩道，約 1962 年。

電車的左方為於 1940 年落成的消防局。右方為 1947 年開業的英男茶樓，其樓下之德豐隆米店左面，可見堅拿寶靈頓運河明渠之石圍欄。該明渠約於 1970 年被蓋平。後來，這一帶即成為「打小人」勝地。左中部可見大丸百貨的招牌。

Hennessy Road, c. 1962. The fire station built in 1940 is on the left. The stone fence of the canal on Canal Road can be seen on the right.

23 羅素街電車廠，約 1975 年。

背後可見堅拿道西的樓宇。右方為羅素街。電車廠於 1980 年代後期遷往石塘咀，原址改建為時代廣場。

The tram depot on Russell Street and Canal Road East, Causwway Bay, c. 1975. The depot was rebuilt into Times Square in early 1990s.

 約 1925 年的跑馬地。

　　右中部山坡下端是已改為「香江養和院」(養和醫院) 的原愉園遊樂場。正中一列房屋的背後是歷史悠久的黃泥涌村。1930 年，政府清拆黃泥涌村，在此開闢包括山村道、山光道及奕蔭街等多條街道，此一帶亦發展為高尚住宅區。當時，電車經天樂里等右方道路進出跑馬地。

The Happy Valley Racecourse, c. 1925. The Wong Nai Chung Village is behind those four-storey residential houses. The village was redeveloped into high class residential area in 1930.

約 1986 年的跑馬地。

中前方為養和醫院、山村道及電車總站。右中部仍見禮頓山上的政府宿舍，其旁邊可見興利中心及世貿中心等新型建築。

Panoramic view of Happy Valley, c. 1986.

 銅鑼灣迴旋處的電車總站，約 1925 年。

有密封電車及木頂篷電車各一輛，左邊是古典候車亭。背後為 1916 年由灣仔「大佛口」遷至此的法國聖保祿女書院及醫院。這一帶之前是渣甸紡織廠。

Two trams, one with a wooden top and another fully enclosed, parked at the Causeway Bay tram roundabout, c. 1925. The Saint Paul's Convent School and Hospital are at the back.

 維多利亞公園年宵市場，約 2005 年。

年宵市場於 1960 年起在維多利亞公園內舉辦。在此之前，年宵市場開設於附近的興發街、留仙街、歌頓道及威非路道一帶。

Lunar New Year Fair at Victoria Park, c. 2005.

25
26 | 27

南全景水棚水華　SOUTH CHINA BATHING BEACH H.K.

28 筲箕灣道上的單軌電車路，約 1905 年。

　　該電車路段位於北角名園遊樂場附近，覓得波酒店 (Metropole Hotel) 旁的筲箕灣道 (1936 年易名英皇道) 之七姊妹泳灘區。電車路上舖有雙軌避車處以方便對頭電車通過。

The single-track tramway on Shau Kei Wan Road (renamed as King's Road in 1936), beside the Tsat Tsz Mui beach area, c. 1905.

29 北角七姊妹泳灘區的南華會游水棚，約 1933 年。

　　除南華會和若干家體育會外，亦有多家百貨公司在此設立泳棚。圖左可見一往來此區的專線電車。前方為健康村的稻田。這一帶於 1954 年開始平整，由香港平民屋宇有限公司發展為共有 600 個單位的健康村「平民屋」(廉租屋)。

South China Bathing Beach, in front of the Healthy Valley, Tsat Tsz Mui, North Point, c. 1933.

30 西灣河筲箕灣道，約 1954 年。

　　左方為太富街，正中為位於 38 至 40 號的永平百貨公司。迄至 1950 年代初，西灣河及筲箕灣仍為「自給自足」的社區。典型的三層高唐樓之住客，不少為太古船塢職工。因交通不便，「上」環 (意指前往中環) 被視作「大事」。約 1950 年時，仍有渡輪前往中環，以補電車及巴士的不足。

The three-storey residential houses in early 1950's on Shau Kei Wan Road, Sai Wan Ho. Tai Foo Street is on the left.

28 | 29
———
30

 由成安街望向西灣河，約 1953 年。

　　右方為於 1872 年建成的舊筲箕灣街市，所在現為西灣河文娛中心。其背後是太古員工宿舍太安樓，後於 1968 年改建成同名住宅大廈。太古宿舍羣背後可見太古船塢的「天秤」(吊臂)。左方三層高唐樓羣的住客除了太古船塢員工外，亦有不少漁民。該處大部分店舖為民生所需如米舖、雜貨舖及藥材舖等。

Sai Wan Ho district, looking west from Shing On Street, c. 1953. The Taikoo Dockyard and the lifting arms and cranes can be seen at the centre.

筲箕灣愛秩序灣避風塘及漁港，約 1960 年。

其背後為金華街、望隆街及筲箕灣東大街一帶。對上山段曾有一條綠寶村，後於 1960 年代建成大型屋邨明華大廈。這裏為香港早期工業區之一，於 1920 年代已有膠鞋、五金及食品等工廠。

Typhoon shelter and fishing port in Aldrich Bay, Shau Kei Wan, c. 1960.

 約 1920 年，筲箕灣漁港全景。

正中為多座太古船塢員工宿舍。當年，筲箕灣仍有「餓人灣」的別名。

Panoramic view of Aldrich Bay, Shau Kei Wan, c. 1920.

 位於筲箕灣東大街尾譚公廟道的譚公廟，約 1950 年。

譚公廟於 1905 年落成，當中亦供奉西湖靈隱寺的濟顛（濟公）活佛，曾於 2002 年重修。長久以來，譚公廟與附近的天后廟和城隍廟，一直香火鼎盛。

Tam Kung Temple in Shau Kei Wan, c. 1950.

32 | 33
34

278

Shaukiwan Bay, Hong-Kong

57 CHINESS TEMPLE H K.

- 香港政府憲報

- 《循環日報》

- 《華字日報》

- 《華僑日報》

- 《星島日報》

- 《華僑日報》編印：《香港年鑑》(1947-1993)

- E. J. Eitel, *Europe in China: The History of Hong Kong from the Beginning to the Year 1882*, Kelly & Walsh Co., 1895.

- 何其銳先生

- 陳創楚先生

- 謝炳奎先生

- 麥勵濃先生

- 香港大學圖書館